Don Underwood

PRAY LIKE JESUS

Rediscovering the Lord's Prayer

D0101683

Abingdon Press / Nashville

PRAY LIKE JESUS
Rediscovering the Lord's Prayer

Copyright © 2017 by Don Underwood
All rights reserved.

This book is printed on elemental chlorine-free paper.

Library of Congress Cataloging-in-Publication data applied for.

ISBN 978-1-5018310-5-8

Scripture quotations are taken from the New Revised Standard Version of the Bible, copyright 1989, Division of Christian Education of the National Council of the Churches of Christ in the United States of America. Used by permission. All rights reserved.

17 18 19 20 21 22 23 24 25 26 — 10 9 8 7 6 5 4 3 2 1

MANUFACTURED IN THE UNITED STATES OF AMERICA

For Baba

Contents

Introduction **9**
The Best-Known Prayer in the World

The Lord's Prayer **15**

1. On Our Knees **17**
"Our Father, who art in heaven, hallowed be thy name."

2. What Would Jesus Do? **33**
"Thy kingdom come, thy will be done on earth as it is in heaven."

3. Daily Food **53**
"Give us this day our daily bread."

4. How Can God Forgive Us? **71**
"And forgive us our trespasses . . ."

5. The Unforgiven **89**
". . . as we forgive those who trespass against us."

6. Tempted by What? **107**
"And lead us not into temptation, but deliver us from evil."

Notes **126**

Acknowledgments **127**

Introduction

The Best-Known Prayer in the World

They saw him out there every morning, on his knees, early, as the sun rose in the east. Until he had come along, their understanding of prayer had revolved around what they had heard from the Pharisees: loud, long, self-righteous, and self-serving. But he was different. He could spend hours at a time in silence, as if he were listening more than asking. And when he rose from his prayers and joined them for the day's work, he seemed to be powerfully energized while also utterly at peace. There was an unmistakable and unique quality to this man they called Jesus, and the longer they stayed with him the more they suspected that it was rooted in his practice of daily prayer. So one day they asked him, "Teach us to pray."

And he did. Matthew records the moment:

"Our Father in heaven,
hallowed be your name.
Your kingdom come.
Your will be done,
on earth as it is in heaven.
Give us this day our daily bread.
And forgive us our debts,
as we also have forgiven our debtors.
And do not bring us to the time of trial,
but rescue us from the evil one."

(Matthew 6:9-13)

The most famous prayer in the world can be recited in less than thirty seconds, and it is a virtual treasure of theological and spiritual insight. There are 2.1 billion Christians in the world, and most of them know this prayer by heart. And yet the power of the prayer has been lost in our generation.

When was the last time you recited the Lord's Prayer? Perhaps it was at a worship service following the pastoral prayer, or maybe at a recent wedding. Maybe you can't even remember the last time you said it. And yet, the saying of the Lord's Prayer is one of the most explicit instructions that Jesus gives us in the New Testament. It is one of the simplest ways that we can practice being a follower of his.

The most famous prayer in the world is remarkably simple and brief. A four-year-old child can, with a little practice, memorize it. Most Christians know it by heart and can easily recite it. In fact, that might be part of the problem: it is so well known and easily recited that most of us never even think about the words as we rattle them off silently or in a corporate worship setting. The thesis of this book is that the Lord's Prayer is both an insightful theological statement and, if recited daily, a powerful means by which one can develop a rich devotional life.

For the last several years, after a lifetime of saying it only sporadically, I have recited the Lord's Prayer on a daily basis. I have also spent some time unpacking the theological and existential power of the prayer. Recently I preached a series of sermons on the Lord's Prayer, and each week I was amazed at how much power and insight can be found in each of the phrases that make up its content. I also received enthusiastic feedback from parishioners who adopted the habit of saying it on a daily basis as a spiritual discipline. Church members still approach me to offer a word of thanks for encouraging them in this daily spiritual practice.

When we look carefully at the content of the prayer, we discover that it provides rich spiritual guidance for nearly every personality: for contemplatives searching for a deeper spiritual life; for the person who is passionate about social justice; for those seeking the strength to simply make it through another day. It is all there in the Lord's Prayer, providing a simple but brilliant holistic approach to the relationship between God and believer. In fewer than seventy words Jesus remarkably covers the breadth of the Christian message and experience: our relationship to God, our mission from God, our source of strength and power for daily living, our daily reminder of the importance of confession and forgiveness, and a hopeful refrain that commits us to the understanding that the future belongs not to us, but to God.

Three years ago I began experimenting with a number of spiritual disciplines, especially meditation and contemplative prayer. I am a type A personality, and had you asked a few years earlier if I would ever consider adopting a spiritual discipline that involves meditation, I would have laughed at you. I assure you that none of my friends or colleagues would have been able to see me in that role. But when life gets tough, and the twists and turns of the journey become frightening or lonesome or overwhelmingly sad, the sojourner becomes ever more creative and courageous— even desperate—to find both spiritual power and peace. At a tough moment in my journey I received an e-mail from a young man in my church who had survived cancer when in his twenties. Bright, athletic, gifted, and extroverted, he did not fit my image of a contemplative. But I knew he had adopted meditation as a daily practice, and I knew it had been a transforming discipline for him. I am thirty years his elder, but I credit him with teaching me and leading me into a daily discipline upon which I now depend.

Please know that I am a novice at contemplative practice, and I encourage you to read many other authors who have devoted lifetimes to it. But throughout this book I will offer ideas and suggestions about how you can "stretch" the Lord's

Prayer by using contemplative images and metaphors, and also how the Lord's Prayer can be used to guide you into a deeper and more meaningful devotional life. At the close of each chapter you'll find a section called "Spiritual Reflection," in which I share a few ideas about ways in which spiritual practice and the Lord's Prayer can be mutually reinforcing. In these sections, I tend to use the term *spiritual practice* rather than *spiritual discipline* because I think it captures the attitude that works best for most of us. Discipline implies a kind of Spartan self-denial, whereas practice summons the idea that we can grow better over time. Practice acknowledges that we are mere amateurs attempting to grow and progress. Hopefully, like the child who joyfully practices baseball or swimming, we will come to eagerly anticipate our times of spiritual practice.

In each of these sections I will share a word about my personal experience with spiritual practice, and then make suggestions about linking one's devotional time with the particular phrase from the Lord's Prayer that was discussed in the chapter. Our goal will be to discuss each phrase of the Lord's Prayer in a way that connects the existential challenges of everyday life with the profound biblical and theological insights that are the buried treasure of the prayer, and then suggest ways of mining those insights for a richer and deeper spiritual life. The reader will discover throughout the book what I call a holistic approach to the prayer. We will deal with not only biblical and spiritual themes, but will borrow occasionally from the discipline of psychotherapy in an effort to address our natural human yearning for spiritual and emotional thriving.

While the individual reader might use this book in a number of different ways—theological primer, encouragement for the devotional life, a catalyst for considering significant personal changes—I am confident that it will also be useful in group settings. Sunday school classes, Bible studies, and other small groups will find powerful biblical themes to probe and discuss. There are chapters in the second half of the book where I attempt to tackle some daunting theological doctrines such as original sin, the biblical concept of daily bread, and St. Paul's understanding of grace. I trust this material will enrich the lively theological and biblical discussions of any small group or class. I am also hopeful that this book will encourage the members of small groups in the discipline of holding one another accountable for daily spiritual practice and the reciting of the prayer. My loftiest vision would be that the book would play a small role in revitalizing the spiritual lives of some of the 2.1 billion Christians around the world, and that we would move one step closer to that state of grace that Jesus described as the kingdom of God on earth.

The Lord's Prayer

Throughout this book I will be using the version of the Lord's Prayer with which I grew up. There are other versions of the prayer, and I encourage readers to recite and meditate on the one they appreciate the most.

Our Father, who art in heaven,
  hallowed be thy name.
  Thy kingdom come,
  thy will be done on earth as it is
  in heaven.
Give us this day our daily bread.
And forgive us our trespasses,
  as we forgive those who trespass
  against us.
And lead us not into temptation,
  but deliver us from evil.
For thine is the kingdom, and the power,
and the glory,
  forever. Amen.[1]

1

On Our Knees

Our Father, who art in heaven,
hallowed be thy name.

There is a wonderful story, probably apocryphal, about two of the greatest Texas ranchers of the late nineteenth and early twentieth century. Burk Burnett was the owner and operator of a vast cattle empire whose crown jewel was the legendary Four Sixes Ranch. Tom Waggoner owned the equally prestigious Waggoner Ranch and in the last part of his life was a prominent entrepreneur and businessman in Fort Worth. The two men were friends but also deeply competitive, and sometimes an argument would break out that would conclude with a sizable wager.

One day the conversation turned to religion, and Mr. Waggoner challenged Mr. Burnett: "Burk, I bet you can't even recite the Lord's Prayer." Mr. Burnett retorted by offering a $50 bet, and a cowboy was summoned to hold the money. Mr. Burnett confidently began his prayer in a solemn tone: "Now I lay me down to sleep, I pray the Lord my soul to keep..." Mr. Waggoner stopped him by turning to the cowboy and saying, "Hell, he knows it. Pay him his fifty dollars."

I've always appreciated that story, not only for its humor but also because it offers a cautionary word about the dangers of being too sure of ourselves when it comes to spiritual matters. It is a reminder that, when it comes to religion, none of us knows as much as we think we know. Though the New Testament is full of warnings about the dangers of self-righteousness and judgmental attitudes, the world of religion continues to be plagued by a lack of humility, both intellectual and spiritual. The Lord's Prayer, said daily and thoughtfully, begins by placing us in the proper relationship with the first member of the Trinity, God the Father, and then it proceeds to provide a remarkably concise theological articulation of what it means to be a follower of Jesus.

The Original Prayer

When one looks at the primary scriptural reference for the Lord's Prayer in the sixth chapter of Matthew, it becomes clear that Jesus taught his prayer to the disciples in the context of his teaching about humility. In his introduction to the prayer, Jesus clearly draws a contrast between the superficial, boastful spirituality of the Pharisees and the kind of humble spirituality he was trying to model for his followers:

> *And whenever you pray, do not be like the*
> *hypocrites; for they love to stand and pray*
> *in the synagogues and at the street corners,*
> *so that they may be seen by others. Truly I*
> *tell you, they have received their reward. But*
> *whenever you pray, go into your room and*
> *shut the door and pray to your Father who is*
> *in secret; and your Father who sees in secret*
> *will reward you.*
>
> *When you are praying, do not heap up empty*
> *phrases as the Gentiles do; for they think*
> *that they will be heard because of their many*
> *words. Do not be like them, for your Father*
> *knows what you need before you ask him.*
>
> *Pray then in this way . . .*
>
> (Matthew 6:5-9)

It would be wrong to interpret this passage as a prohibition against public prayer. It is rather a warning about self-serving prayer. Throughout the New Testament we see the ongoing critique that Jesus aims squarely at the religious leaders of the day, primarily the Pharisees. Jesus did not condemn the Pharisees for their knowledge or their piety, but rather for the self-righteousness and the self-serving rigidity with which they interpreted the Jewish law. Jesus considered the spirituality of the Pharisees to be not only empty and hypocritical but also abusive of those who had less education and power.

When Jesus advises his followers that proper prayer can be simple and concise, with a minimum of words, he is empowering all the people of God. He is, in effect, telling them that the barriers of class, education, money, and power that kept them on the periphery of society have no standing with God.

What a revolutionary idea it must have been for the common people to hear from Jesus that their words and phrases could be more powerful expressions of prayer than the learned and elaborate words of their religious leaders! This abolishing of the religious, institutional, and hierarchical barriers between God and God's people is an ongoing theme of the Gospels and, in this context, the Lord's Prayer becomes an even more compelling expression of the entire ministry of Jesus in turning upside down the cultural and religious assumptions of the day. His teaching of this short, simple, and yet profound prayer is literally an act of liberation and empowerment for all the people of his day and ours.

We will also discover that the prayer is remarkably comprehensive in its theological breadth and depth. When prayed and meditated upon with thoughtfulness and sensitivity, the Lord's Prayer truly becomes a daily catechism that reminds us of many grand truths of the Judeo-Christian faith. Most importantly, however, the Lord's Prayer has the power to transform our spiritual lives on a daily basis. If one prays slowly and thoughtfully, the first phrase alone has the ability to transport us from the dimness and drudgery of everyday life into the serene presence of a magnificent Creator God who loves us and sustains us on a daily basis.

A Transcendent God

I like using metaphors and images to enhance the reciting of the Lord's Prayer, and when saying the opening phrase—"Our Father who art in heaven, hallowed be thy name"—I often take time to remember my first trip to the Grand Canyon. I was twelve years old when my parents told my brothers and me that we were going to Arizona and would see one of the great natural wonders of the world. I remember telling a friend about this with great enthusiasm. He responded by saying that he had been there and that it was very disappointing, nothing more than "a great big hole." That dampened my enthusiasm considerably until, a few weeks later, I stood before the canyon and was overwhelmed by both the grandeur and the beauty of it. Not only did I wonder about the intelligence of anyone who would call it nothing more than a big hole, but I thought, *Who could stand in this place and not believe in God?* In fact, who could stand at the Grand Canyon and not consider God to be both powerful and holy, which is the meaning of that somewhat archaic word *hallowed*? Sometimes I will pray that first phrase in this way: "Our father who art in heaven, holy be your name."

I don't pretend to know the mysteries of creation, but I do know there is a creative force in the universe that utterly dwarfs us and our capacity to understand even ourselves, much less the complexities and paradoxes of everyday existence. Theologians call this a transcendent God, a God who dwells outside the normal experience of mortals. For most of history humans have envisioned a transcendent God as one who resides in "heaven," a kind of physical residence that exists somewhere "up there." I actually love the image, which some might call primitive, of heaven as somewhere in the skies. It is no wonder at all that our early ancestors would look to the skies—the place that holds the sun, the moon, and the stars, and from which comes rain as the gift of life itself—as the home of God. I choose to celebrate that image without taking it too literally. The truth it conveys is that God is Creator, and that God's creative power and unlimited love are beyond the full comprehension or experience of humans.

Calling upon this image of the Grand Canyon, and others like it, helps me to understand the meaning and importance of the first phrase of the Lord's Prayer. I like to take some time and dwell on these images as I ponder the first words of the prayer. I want my mind and heart to become immersed in this image of a transcendent God who has the power to breathe life into the universe and into each and every human being, a God who cares for us and our loved ones more deeply than we can imagine.

Either God Is or God Isn't

The seeds of this book were probably planted early one morning several years ago. I was struggling with intense anxiety and worry about a challenge I was dealing with. I had, frankly, exhausted my mental and emotional resources in my efforts to personally "fix" this particular situation. I was beaten, with no place to turn. In a spirit of desperation more than anything else, I fell to my knees and began to say the Lord's Prayer. The words *Our Father, who art in heaven, hallowed be thy name* echoed in my brain as if I were hearing them for the very first time. I stopped at that phrase and continued to think and meditate upon it. I was seized by the thought that either God is or God isn't. If God is, then God is indeed in heaven, is the creator of all there is, and is the lover and sustainer of all there is, including me and the ones I care about. Suddenly, in a moment of powerful grace, all the anxiety drained from my spirit and my body, and I "gave" this situation to God in an act of utter and complete trust. I confessed my personal inability to control the outcome of these circumstances, and I experienced a remarkable kind of serenity as I left it in the hands of God. The words *Our Father, who art in heaven, hallowed be thy name* had, quite literally, led me to a moment of spiritual transformation and emotional healing, and suddenly I understood the power of this prayer to change lives. I have prayed it consistently from that moment on.

That particular experience was so enlightening to me that it has become a consistent theme in my preaching over the past few years. Occasionally someone will say to me, "We're here. We're in church. Obviously, we believe in God!" I would say there is a difference between having an intellectual belief that there is a God and living by an existential awareness that there is a God that fundamentally changes the way one views the world.

All of us must address this question for ourselves, but I confess that unless I begin my day in prayer, giving the day to a transcendent God, I will generally take it back for myself. I won't live the day in denial that there is a God, but I also won't live by the power and freedom that comes with the faith that a loving God cares about me and my work and my life. The phrase "either God is or God isn't" has become the touchstone by which I constantly manage my spiritual life in order to better manage my life as a husband, father, grandfather, and pastor.

When I pray the Lord's Prayer these days, with that constant reminder that either God is or God isn't, I try to dwell long enough on the first phrase that my worries seem trivial, my lack of understanding feels normal, and I eventually find myself "resting" in the confidence that there is a great big God who will one day make sense out of all the nonsense that seems to fill the world. I take time to be grateful for the fact that God sees the suffering and violence of the world, that God knows about my fears and insecurities, and that the God who created the Grand Canyon is the same God who is able to bring resurrection out of death, and hope out of despair.

The first phrase of the Lord's Prayer, and the images I bring to it, force me spiritually to my knees, where I am utterly grateful to be in the position of a supplicant to a great big God who is both creator and sustainer of all there is.

Downsizing God

Far too many of us, including preachers, have responded to the modern, scientific world by downsizing God. By this I mean that, feeling inadequate to respond to the theories of the Big Bang and quantum mechanics, we have deemphasized God as a transcendent creator and simply focused on the teachings of Jesus about being a good neighbor. Confronted by the evangelists of atheism, some of us have chosen to abandon the proclamation of a Big God, a transcendent God who created the universe, in favor of a proclamation that urges us simply to do social work or a proclamation that pontificates about the cultural or moral debates of the moment.

This is not to say that loving and serving our neighbor is not important. In fact, it lies at the center of the gospel. Jesus clearly told us to love God and love our neighbors. He said, "On these two commandments hang all the law and the prophets" (Matthew 22:40). But Jesus always understood and proclaimed this in the context of faith in a transcendent

God who spoke the world into existence and who created our neighbors to be our brothers and sisters. This understanding that we are all the children of God is what animates our passion as Christians to serve others, and it distinguishes what we do from what government or secular agencies do. If we lose the understanding that everything we do should be in grateful response to a creator God, we forfeit not only our passion but also the transforming power of knowing that we are doing not just good work but God's work.

I have a friend who likes to say, "If God is, God is a lot bigger than we thought." I believe that should be our proper response as Christians to the scientific theories of the day. Rather than attacking science, or shrinking in the face of scientific ideas we do not understand, we should view science as that which confronts and expands our concept of God. As our scientific understanding of the universe grows larger, the mysteries of creation have grown more complex. Even the great physicists who claim to be atheists will acknowledge that the universe continues to confront us with mysteries that cannot be fully explained by quantum mechanics and other scientific theories. And research has revealed that a significant percentage of scientists, even at our most elite universities, are people of faith. The first phrase of the Lord's Prayer is a daily reminder that the God we worship is a big and transcendent God, the creator of the universe. We should start each day by embracing the power of that proclamation.

A Selfie Day or the Lord's Day?

We live in a remarkably narcissistic age. A few years ago I was talking with the youth director at our church, and he asked me what I thought was the most common ambition of today's youth. I took some wild guesses: astrophysicist, electrical engineer, doctor, computer programmer. I wasn't even close. It was, he told me, to be famous.

At first I was shocked by that notion, and frankly incredulous. But the more I thought about it, the more it made sense. Today's youth (and their parents and grandparents!) are constantly barraged by television "reality" shows that have made ordinary people famous. A person's popularity and fame can be measured by the number of people who follow them on Twitter. Anyone can upload a YouTube video of themselves with the hope that it will "go viral." For many people, Facebook has become the means by which their personal lives are shared with much of the world, and for some it has become a competition with friends and associates about who leads the most interesting life.

For the first time in history, an ordinary person can send a digital image or text or song into cyberspace and have the potential to reach millions of people. An anonymous but truly talented person could potentially record a song in her bedroom, post it to a media account, and instantly become a star. On the one hand, this is the great democratizing of access to an audience. It can be a powerful way of organizing people or promoting a cause or spreading a message, including the gospel. For example, think about the amazing success of the Ice Bucket Challenge, a campaign to promote awareness of and contributions to the ALS Association. The campaign went viral on social media, demonstrating the power of the Internet to create good works and acts of generosity.

Like all things, however, the Internet can be used for good or evil. Or it can lead to the temptation to be self-serving or narcissistic. And let's be honest: none of us is immune to the seductions of a digital world or the power of social media. By way of personal confession, I write a weekly column that is published as an e-mail. Occasionally, when explaining it to a new acquaintance or church member, I find myself telling them proudly how many people receive it each week. And it would be disingenuous of me to pretend that I wouldn't love for that number to grow exponentially.

And who among us has never sent a selfie? I sometimes say that we are living in a selfie world, one in which even heads of state are photographed with their smart phones aimed at themselves! It seems to me rather remarkable that, without any hint of irony or embarrassment, our culture has so thoroughly embraced the notion of the selfie. Some of us grew up at a time when we were lectured about modesty, both in manners and appearance. Today that seems so quaint, and the selfie rules.

The first phrase of the Lord's Prayer serves as an antidote to our selfie world. It reminds us of a powerful and transcendent and creative God in whose presence we feel small. It places us spiritually on our knees. It encourages us to adopt a spirit of appropriate humility. Every single day each of us makes a decision, either consciously or unconsciously: Will this day belong to me, or will it belong to God? Will it be a selfie day or God's day? Will I live solely for myself, or will I live as a grateful servant of the One who created me? Meditating for a few minutes on the phrase "Our Father who art in heaven, hallowed be thy name" can help us to feel appropriately small in the presence of a big God and to begin our day more faithfully.

Spiritual Reflection:
Experiencing Transcendence

Most of us spend our days and nights imprisoned by those things that have been made by humans: steel and concrete and glass. Even our commutes find us confined in automobiles or trains, surrounded by hundreds of other vehicles, attempting to navigate the endless concrete trails of modern life. Compared with the Old Testament Hebrew nomads who slept and traveled in the open, or even with our nineteenth-century forbears, we are quite challenged in our ability to experience and celebrate the transcendence of a creator God. Our senses, especially those of seeing and hearing, are so overwhelmed by the mundane things we humans have made that we have difficulty perceiving the magnificence of what God has made. Spiritual practice is one of the ways in which we can redirect our attention to the Creator God who spoke the world into existence.

I occasionally will remind members of my congregation of what I call the 20/20 rule: if you will spend at least twenty minutes a day in silence (preferably in the dark) for twenty days in a row, God will show up. That is my way of taking the mystery out of spiritual practice: it is more a matter of persistence than technique. There are lots of spiritual teachers and many ways of practicing spiritual discipline, but the most important thing is to begin! Remember the Chinese proverb that the journey of a thousand miles begins with a single step. I maintain that if one will not obsess about technique, and simply accept the fact that any spiritual practice will be plagued by distractions, there will come a moment within the first twenty days when there will be at least a subtle awareness of the presence of a transcendent God.

I have already referenced in this chapter my experience with visually focusing on the Grand Canyon as an example of God's creativity, but I offer it as merely one example among many. I encourage the reader to explore past experiences that have spoken of creation or of God. Use all your senses, especially vision and hearing. What images speak to you of the magnificence of God? Sometimes we are driven to our knees by the need for forgiveness or the burdens we carry, but what drives you to your knees in awe and thanksgiving of a powerful creator God?

Every summer I go to the beach for a few days because I covet the infinite vista of the far horizon and the sound of pounding waves. If you are a beach person, perhaps that is the kind of image that could be meaningful to you. If you enjoy the mountains, you surely can recall special places that speak to you of God's magnificence. Strive to be as personal as possible, and incorporate those images and sounds into your times of silence and prayer. Then allow the words *Our Father, who art in heaven, hallowed be thy name...*drive you into a place of humility and gratitude. There is no better way to start your day.

2

What Would Jesus Do?

Thy kingdom come,
thy will be done on earth as it is in heaven.

A number of years ago I was scheduled to conduct a January wedding for a young woman in our church who had an identical twin. A few days before Christmas I was shopping in a large discount store and, as I entered a long line to check out, I noticed that one of the twins was the cashier. As the line inched forward, she looked up, noticed me in line, and greeted me warmly. Without guile, and somewhat naively, I responded, "Great to see you! Are you the one I'm supposed to marry in January, or is that your sister?" As soon as those words fell out of my mouth I noticed the widened eyes and incredulous expressions of the shoppers in the line with me. And I will never forget the whispered and exasperated voice of an elderly lady standing just behind me: "My God, what is this world coming to?"

That's a pretty good question, isn't it? I won't use this space to articulate in detail the laundry list of challenges we are now facing in America, not to mention the seemingly endless issues we face as a global community. Between the discovery of new and potentially deadly drug-resistant bacteria at the microscopic level and the testing of ever larger nuclear weapons at the macroscopic level, the viability of the human race appears to be constantly under threat. Wars, terrorism, racial tension, and mental health issues continue to inflame rather than pacify our collective human state of emotions. To make matters worse, there is now widespread skepticism about the effectiveness of our most important institutions, ranging from government to the church. If we listen carefully, we will hear it often in one way or the other: "My God, what is this world coming to?"

Life in Jesus' Time

It is difficult to know how to compare the angst of our current generation with that of the first century, but there can be no ambiguity about the fact that life was difficult for those to whom Jesus ministered. From a global perspective, the historical period recorded by the Gospels took place within the context of the famous Pax Romana. After centuries of war, the defeat of Marc Antony at the Battle of Actium in 31 B.C. by the Roman emperor Augustus ushered in a period of relative peace that lasted more than two centuries. I confess that my review of this history prompted a sense of awe, if not historical jealousy, given the volatile and violent nature of that region in today's world. It should also, however, provide an optimistic perspective. There was nothing in the preceding history in that part of the world that would have prompted one to predict an era of peace. Peace came as the result of visionary and courageous leadership and as a recognition that peace would serve citizens better than the potential risks/rewards of war. Can't we hope and work for the same in our modern historical context?

Having praised Caesar for good work at the global level, we now must calibrate that praise with a description of life on the ground during the time of Jesus. It was a hierarchical world, and while it provided a lavish and peaceful lifestyle for those living at the top of the social ladder, it also meant poverty, disease, and exploitation for noncitizens (which included most Jews) as well as for the poor. When Jesus arrived on the scene, he entered a society in which most Jews were treated harshly by both the Roman authorities and the educated and upwardly mobile Jewish leaders of the Temple. Collusion among the powerful, both Jewish and Roman, at the expense of the poor is one of the central historical themes found in the Gospels. It clearly lies at the heart of the betrayals that took Jesus to the cross. Average Jews found themselves constantly victimized by the taxes and demands of Roman and Jewish overlords. When Jesus used the word *kingdom* in the second part of his prayer, surely it caught the attention of his followers.

Through the years, the church has resorted to various descriptions, some bordering on gaudy, of what God's kingdom in heaven might look like: pearly gates, streets paved with gold, God's elect adorned with angels' wings. However, a fair reading of Jesus' life and teachings provides a more prosaic, but in many ways more powerful, understanding. The kingdom of God in heaven is a place where justice reigns; where all people are treated and loved equally; where there is no abuse by the powerful and no patronizing of the poor; where a person's status is derived from no other fact than being a child of God. The currency in the kingdom of God is, quite simply, the love of God, distributed lavishly and without prejudice upon all those who simply choose to embrace their status as unworthy but grateful recipients of God's grace.

The contrast between that heavenly society and the reality of status-driven worldly society could not be greater. Imagine the joy and anticipation of those who were able to hear and envision this unique promise from a man who seemed to have peeked into the mind of God. And then imagine the response of his followers when he hinted that it is God's intention to make this idyllic kingdom a reality right here on earth! In this line of the Lord's Prayer, Jesus changed the conversation: not "up there" but "down here"!

Pastor and author John Ortberg interprets this passage as follows:

> Many people think our job is to get my after-life destination taken care of, then tread water till we all get ejected and God comes back and torches this place. But Jesus never told any-body—neither his disciples nor us—to pray, "Get me out of here so I can go up there." His prayer was, "Make up there come down here." Make things down here run the way they do up there.[2]

What if we could catch this vision about the kingdom of God and allow it to transform the manner in which we approach our daily lives?

What Would Jesus Do?

A few years ago, wristbands with the initials WWJD became very popular. The letters stood, of course, for "What would Jesus do?" Though I choose not to wear wristbands at all, I like the idea of testing our decisions against the biblical model that Jesus provides for us. So much of the time we are influenced by the observation that "Everyone is doing it." That may be so, but for the Christian, the pivotal question really is "What would Jesus do?"

When we come to this part of the Lord's Prayer—"Thy kingdom come. Thy will be done on earth as it is in heaven."—we receive enormous clarity about the vision Jesus had for our communal life on earth. We don't have to wonder what Jesus would do, because he gave us explicit instructions about what to do. I like to refer to this part of the prayer as the vision and mission statement for the Christian life. Jesus taught and preached about the kingdom of God more than any other subject, and in this prayer he makes it clear that our mission is to live life on earth in a way that reflects the kingdom of God in heaven.

If we take this part of the prayer with utter seriousness, it is likely to change our theological perspective in some ways. Many Christians remain solely focused on the rewards of heaven as opposed to the trials on earth. Some expressions of Christianity emphasize almost exclusively the evangelical call to "make sure you are going to heaven." There is, of course, nothing wrong with being comforted by the great promise of our faith that God is both Alpha and Omega, and that one day

> *He will wipe every tear from their eyes.*
> *Death will be no more;*
> *mourning and crying and pain will be no more,*
> *for the first things have passed away.*
>
> (Revelation 21:4)

This passage reflects the hope and promise of our faith. But this great eschatological vision of God's future should not only reassure but also motivate people of faith. If we fully trust that the final outcome of history is in the hands of a loving God, it's easier for us to make daily decisions about how we will do our part to make the kingdom of God in heaven become the kingdom of God on earth.

Live Each Day with Purpose

I have referred to this part of the prayer as the "vision and mission statement" for the Christian life. One of the things we have learned about institutional behavior in recent years is that companies and organizations that have truly functional mission statements perform at a much higher level than those for whom the mission statement is simply a plaque hanging on the boardroom wall or the obligatory statement in the "About Us" page on the website. When organizations have compelling and functional mission statements and when their leaders remain laser-focused on them, employees or volunteers tend to be highly motivated. This is especially true when the mission statement is tied to a vision about how the work of the organization or company can make the world a better place. In those work environments, people tend to show up for work with extra passion and energy. They may value the fact that they get paid for their work, but they experience extra "compensation" in the knowledge that their skills, time, and commitment will make a contribution to the greater good. Every company or organization needs a compelling mission statement. Every church needs one. And guess what? Every person needs one as well.

Regardless of where one works or volunteers, the Lord's Prayer is a call to every single one of us to live each day with passion and purpose. It is a mission statement that is as clear and compelling as one can get, and yet it can be lived out in a multitude of ways. If one begins every day with a commitment to make God's kingdom in heaven become God's kingdom on earth, think of the vast array of opportunities that will present themselves. Regardless of where you work or spend your time, your mission statement can be lived out in many different ways. Let me offer just three simple examples that are based in specific Scriptures.

Radical Hospitality

There is a great story in all three of the synoptic Gospels (Matthew, Mark, and Luke) about how Jesus, though surrounded by many people who were pressing in on him and demanding his attention, sensed the presence of a sick woman who was touching his garment. As soon as she touched him, she was healed of a hemorrhage that had plagued her for twelve years. The best part of the story is that Jesus, busy as he was, stopped everything he was doing and greeted her, in the process providing yet another kind of healing for her. In that moment, for that woman, heaven came down to earth in the simple, kind act of a caring human being. By taking time out of a whirlwind schedule, Jesus conveyed to her that she was important; that she was a valued child of God.

Whether you drive a bus or run a corporation, taking the time to be a caring presence for someone in need is a powerful way of bringing God's heavenly love and acceptance to an earthly companion who perhaps is feeling lost or neglected. For most of us, a day never passes when we don't have the opportunity to reach out and touch another person with a little extra compassion or sensitivity.

A number of years ago a pastor friend shared with me that standing and singing the Lord's Prayer had become a sacred tradition in all their worship services. The members always held hands during this special and moving time. One day an older widow who was in church every single Sunday told my pastor friend that her favorite time of the week was singing the Lord's Prayer because "it is the only time in the week that another human being touches me." Think about that. Sometimes reaching out to another human being is literally being the Christ to them. It is an act of making the kingdom of God in heaven become the kingdom of God on earth. And anyone can do it!

Caring for Those in Need

There is a famous passage about the early days of the church in the final words of Acts 2:

> *They devoted themselves to the apostles'*
> *teaching and fellowship, to the breaking of*
> *bread and the prayers.*

*Awe came upon everyone, because many
wonders and signs were being done by the
apostles. All who believed were together and
had all things in common; they would sell
their possessions and goods and distribute
the proceeds to all, as any had need. Day by
day, as they spent much time together in the
temple, they broke bread at home and ate
their food with glad and generous hearts,
praising God and having the goodwill of all
the people. And day by day the Lord added
to their number those who were being saved.*
(Acts 2:42-47)

That passage lays out a compelling vision for Christian community, which is mutual accountability for the welfare of all. The passage implies that some had prospered more than others, but they shared their blessings with all who were in need. They all lived out of a sense of abundance, and mutual sharing became a source of great communal joy. They shared meals and possessions, joys and sorrows, work and leisure. This particular passage is perhaps the ideal—the apex of Christian community—but it is a vision that is alive and vibrant wherever the church and its members are committed to helping those in need. It is one of the ways that the kingdom of God in heaven becomes the kingdom of God on earth.

When Hurricane Katrina hit New Orleans in August 2005, our church in Plano, Texas, more than five hundred miles away, offered to receive evacuees who had no place to go. I will never forget the night they stepped off the bus, carrying their only belongings in black trash bags. A number of them were wearing the same clothes they had on when they escaped the floodwaters of New Orleans, and I could not help but notice the chest-high water lines on some of their shirts. They had been on a bus for over twenty-four hours, their bodies were exhausted, and their eyes were blank and hopeless. But the members of our church sprang into action. Grace and compassion encompassed every step they took toward the evacuees as the church members fulfilled their roles as workers for the Kingdom.

We had just completed construction of a Christian Life Center, complete with a gymnasium, kitchen, and showers. We had wonderful plans about how to use that building, including a contemporary worship service that had started meeting in the gym on Sunday mornings. Our leaders, huddled together in an emergency meeting, quickly concluded that God knew better than we concerning the best and highest use of that building. A unanimous vote canceled the next few worship services, and what we called Hotel Katrina was constructed almost overnight. Gifted lay leaders created the equivalent of a hotel with laundry services, food services, social services, transportation, security, and the like.

There is not space to tell the full story of Hotel Katrina, but I will offer two conversations that convey the spirit of what happened. That first night, when the committee in charge of food services began their planning, there was robust discussion of the best way to serve the meals. There was general consensus on setting up a buffet, until one member of the committee said, "These people have been on their feet for days. I think we should serve sit-down meals." Our men's group was called in, and for days they served as waiters. Not one evacuee ever had to leave a table to get a beverage or a second helping of food.

Hotel Katrina remained open for many weeks. One day after it closed, I was conversing with a friend and church member who had been a nearly round-the-clock volunteer, and this is what he told me: "Don, for years I have faithfully attended Sunday school and church, but I never really understood the gospel until Hotel Katrina. I went up there one night just out of curiosity, but then I was hooked. Once I started volunteering, I rarely left. It was the most life-changing thing that ever happened to me."

To one degree or another, I would say that was true for all of us. Hotel Katrina changed our church. We have never really been the same. Looking back on that experience, we were just doing small things to make the kingdom of God in heaven become the kingdom of God on earth, but in the process we discovered the true joy of Christian community. Some of those New Orleans evacuees decided to stay and are members of our church.

Today the church in America is much maligned in many quarters, and often the criticism is justified. But the church is the only organization in the world whose sole mission is to share the love of God freely, and participating in the mission of the church is one of the most powerful ways in which an individual can live out a personal commitment to make the kingdom of God a reality here on earth.

Sacrificial Witness

In Acts 16 there is a story about Paul and Silas being thrown into prison for preaching the gospel. When night came, a violent earthquake shook the foundation of the prison so hard that the doors flew open and the chains fell from the prisoners. The Roman jailer was awakened and, seeing the opened doors, assumed his prisoners had escaped. In fear of his superiors, he pulled out his sword and prepared to commit suicide rather than face the consequences, but Paul stopped the jailer and assured him that no one had taken advantage of the situation. This self-sacrificial act on the part of Paul was so meaningful to the Roman soldier that he went home and got his family, and they all converted to become followers of Jesus. In the jailer we find the portrait of a man who knew nothing about power other than the power of empire, but in the witness of Paul he discovered the power of love and the majestic generosity of God.

As difficult as it is to admit, most people in our world experience only the "power of empire." In other words, in most places and with most people, power is defined by who is stronger, bigger, meaner, wealthier, or more brutal. This kind of power is experienced in many ways, from aggressive driving on the interstate to the dog-eat-dog competition of the workplace; from the vicious social environment of a middle school to the limited options faced by those who are fleeing oppression or war; from those who live in neighborhoods or homes with modest social and educational capital to those whose lives are constantly haunted by prejudice of one kind or another. In all these examples, power is experienced as oppressive rather than liberating; as selfish and self-serving rather than generous; as a zero-sum game where there are winners and losers. The kingdom of God about which Jesus preached, and which is promised in biblical passages that speak of heaven, turns all those worldly definitions upside down. Power is redefined as God's gracious and generous activity, oftentimes through the work and witness of those who follow Jesus.

I have a friend whose passion for educating children, especially those who face limited opportunities, just radiates from her personality. It is amazing to watch the transformation that takes place when she meets a child (and oftentimes a parent) for the first time. Quite often it is a child with learning challenges or a child who has failed in school because of a deficit in social skills. Often the parent or parents lack the knowledge and experience to advocate for their child, and the future looks bleaker than the past.

The handwriting appears to be on the wall: this child will probably never graduate from high school, resulting in a higher possibility of poverty, addiction, and incarceration. And then my friend enters their lives, and she treats each person with a kind of dignity and respect they have never experienced. She lights up with joy when she interacts with the child, and she instills confidence in the parents about their capacity to help their child personally and by advocating for the child in the school environment. With self-sacrificial generosity of spirit, she turns the power equation upside down. Like the Roman jailer, the people she helps suddenly sense that the power of love and generosity can be greater than the power of empire or social status or educational accomplishment. They experience the power of hope.

My friend has discovered her purpose in life, and she lives it out every day. Her purpose reminds us that opportunities beckon to you and me as well, and we have numerous ways to demonstrate God's love on a daily basis. We can yield to the aggressive driver and wave generously rather than honking or competing; we can do transformational work in our places of employment by treating every person with respect and generosity; we can find places of service where we make a difference in the life of a child or a homeless person or one who has experienced abuse. We can demonstrate the power of God's love by living generously and graciously amid the many whose experience of power has been primarily as victims. Like Paul and the Roman jailer, we can open the door to a new life and new way of seeing things for those who have not experienced the abundance of God's love.

The Big Payoff

While many of us, especially in the United States, enjoy lives of privilege when it comes to the material blessings of life, the quest for meaning, purpose, and joy can be an ongoing challenge. Unfortunately, a higher standard of living does not mitigate the dangers posed by addiction, depression, anxiety, or even sheer boredom. As a pastor I know that most people struggle on a daily basis with some kind of personal challenge, and every person struggles at one time or another. Even those who have been blessed by good genes, good luck, and balanced lifestyles (translation: a minimum of mental or emotional challenges) experience times of loss, illness, and grief. The challenges of maintaining a good marriage or raising healthy children or remaining sane in what appears to be an irrational and violent world are ongoing, even for those who are well equipped to deal with stress and sadness. But here is good news: the mission statement that is found in the Lord's Prayer can lead us toward more holistic, integrated, passionate, and joyful lives. Going the second mile to offer radical hospitality or to care for those in need or to offer a sacrificial witness may be an act of self-giving, but it is also an act that is consistent with one's own self-interest.

It would be utterly irresponsible for me to suggest that serving in a ministry for the homeless or tutoring a child can cure depression or addiction or any other kind of mental or emotional challenge. I am a critic of preachers who suggest that all you have to do is give your life to Christ and smile when you get up in the morning in order for God to bless you with good health and abundant riches. Overpromising the immediate rewards of a faithful lifestyle is a mistake and a disservice to those who are struggling. But on the other hand, it is absolutely true that a conscious commitment to purposeful living can amplify the joy one finds in daily life. A focus on others rather than self can deepen one's compassion and help clarify one's personal mission in life. A daily choice to help the kingdom of God in heaven become the kingdom of God on earth can enrich any life with deeper meaning and greater joy. Reciting and living out the Lord's Prayer on a daily basis is not only a way of living faithfully; it is also a way of embracing the abundance, hope, and joy that is offered by walking with Christ.

Spiritual Reflection:
A Call to Action

I have to confess that for years I avoided any kind of spiritual practice that could be labeled as "contemplative." In my mind that word represented a kind of spirituality that retreats from the world, a kind of piety that embraces reclusiveness rather than action. As an idealistic type A, I was out to change the world, not run from it. I viewed the post-Resurrection disciples as followers of Jesus whose passion for the gospel literally altered the course of history. I wanted to stand in that tradition, a person of action whose decision to follow Jesus meant a life committed to building up the church and the kingdom of God.

Not long after developing a consistent routine of morning prayer and meditation, I signed up for daily e-mails from Richard Rohr's Center for Action and Contemplation. I immediately noticed, of course, the implications of the name of his organization. At one time, a center for "action and contemplation" would have seemed incongruous to me, but no longer. I was already noticing the surprising impact of contemplative practice: it was leading me to greater clarity about my mission in life, and increased energy and focus in pursuing it. Surprisingly, rather than tempting me into a life of passivity, it was urging me forward into a life of increased activity. This in spite of the fact that I was routinely finishing my periods of meditation with a kind of serenity and peacefulness that bordered on mellowness. Even today I don't fully understand this seeming contradiction, but I certainly can testify to the fact that contemplative practice engenders activity, not passivity.

All of this leads to a deeper understanding of Jesus' spirituality. When one reads the Gospels, it is clear that Jesus was a person of enormous energy and vitality. His daily schedule during his three-year ministry must have been exhausting, and yet through it all he remained peaceful and energetic. What was his secret? He knew how to withdraw from the "busy-ness" of life and pray.

There is a fascinating verse stuck right in the middle of the sixth chapter of Luke. Jesus had just healed the withered hand of a man in the synagogue, thereby outraging the authorities. Then, in verse 12, we are told, "Now during those days he went out to the mountain to pray; and he spent the night in prayer to God." Verse 13 then begins a narrative about Jesus choosing his disciples. It is rather remarkable: wedged in between two very significant times of action in the ministry of Jesus, we find this one simple verse telling us about his retreat for a time of prayer. Can there be any doubt that prayer was not just a time of peaceful communion with God, but also a time when God stoked the fires of his spirit and his mission in life?

I have offered in this chapter the idea that the second part of the Lord's Prayer is the "mission statement" of the Christian life, along with some examples about how that mission might be lived out. Let me now encourage the reader to spend some quality prayer time in contemplation of the words *Thy kingdom come, thy will be done....* Now is the time to be extremely personal in consideration of those words. What might they mean in the context of your job, your daily routine, your friends and associates? Is it possible that, when Jesus prayed, he asked a simple question: "Lord, what would you have me do this day to make your kingdom in heaven become your kingdom on earth?" Praying this second part of the Lord's Prayer in a regular time of daily devotion can lead to a day filled with purposeful and hopeful action rather than anxiety or fatigue or sadness.

3

Daily Food

Give us this day our daily bread.

A friend asked me to meet her for breakfast one day. Over ham and eggs we got caught up on the joys and challenges and headaches we were each facing. It was, as always, a very candid and honest conversation. As we were nearing the end of our time together, I asked her a quite personal question: "Abbie, how long have you been sober?" She did something I will never forget. She reached into her purse, pulled out her smartphone, and tapped an app. "Here," she said, "it keeps track for me." I looked at the screen of her phone, and there was a simple number: 7,470. I knew exactly what it meant. She had been sober for 7,470 days.

The way she answered that question makes a difference. She could have said that she had been sober for more than twenty years. But that really would not have captured the way in which she thinks about life nor the method by which she has maintained sobriety over all those years. More than twenty years ago she had gone to her knees one morning and prayed this simple prayer: "Lord, please keep me sober *today*." The next morning she had done the same thing. And then a third morning. For 7,470 days she had started her morning with the same routine: "Lord, please keep me sober *today*." Ask any person who is in recovery, and they will tell you that the secret to sobriety is living as faithfully as possible one day at a time.

When Jesus said, "Give us this day our daily bread," he uttered one of the most powerful lines in the New Testament, but it is a sentiment that is deeply rooted in the Old Testament. From that moment in the twelfth chapter of Genesis when God called Abram and Sarai to undertake a journey, the biblical understanding of faith has involved a commitment to trust God one day at a time. In fact, one of the most insightful ways to read the Bible is as God's call to a journey, and this theme can be found throughout the Old Testament in the stories of the patriarchs, the kings, and the prophets. It is continued in the New Testament with the story of Mary and Joseph, and then with the call by Jesus for his disciples to follow him. This third part of the Lord's Prayer articulates the Christian understanding that God does, indeed, give each of us what we need for the journey, but only one day at a time.

Real Food

What is Jesus referring to when he says "daily bread"? We can begin to understand the meaning of that statement when we ponder the fact that daily bread means different things for different people. For instance, when Jesus uttered those words there were surely people within hearing distance who struggled to find enough food just to survive each day—people who were physically hungry, undernourished, perhaps even starving. We have already talked about the injustice and the crushing poverty that many people found themselves in during the time of Jesus. For those who are searching for their next meal, the words *give us this day our daily bread* have literal meaning. Unfortunately, here we are two thousand years later, and there are still people for whom daily bread is a matter of physical survival.

In the United States, people generally don't starve to death, but that doesn't mean that every person has enough to eat, or that there are no parents who worry about finding enough food to keep their families healthy. Ask teachers who serve in a district where there is poverty, and they will tell you about students who have difficulty concentrating because of poor nutrition. Excellence in early childhood education is one of our greatest challenges these days, and part of the answer is ensuring that every child has access to adequate nutrition.

Not long ago my wife visited one of our grandsons, Liam, at his elementary school and had the opportunity to join him and his friends in the cafeteria for lunch. She was shocked and disturbed when she noticed that one of Liam's friends had no food and no money for lunch. This was in a school that is not located in an area of deep poverty. It is a reminder that far too many people, when they hear the words *daily bread*, immediately think about real food and the desire to eliminate the ache they feel in their stomachs.

Spiritual Food

The problem for many of us is just the opposite. We stuff so many calories in our mouths every day that some of us are killing ourselves with food. Sometimes I will catch myself saying, "I'm starving to death." Perhaps you do the same thing on occasion. Think about how absurd that statement is. Most of us are quite literally eating ourselves to death! But that doesn't mean we aren't starving. Sometimes the more we have to meet our material and physical needs, the more starved we are spiritually. If we expand our understanding of daily bread to include mental, emotional, and spiritual resources, I don't believe there is a single person anywhere in the world for whom this phrase is not powerful and relevant. Each one of us awakens every single day to face real challenges and deal with significant pain or grief. What could be more powerful than the promise of a transcendent God who will give us the spiritual strength and resources to meet those needs on a daily basis?

Some thirty years ago a group of high school seniors sat in my living room one evening as we celebrated their upcoming graduation. This was a yearly event that I enjoyed with the seniors, and I always went around the room and asked them to share their hopes and dreams about the future. This was a particularly bright and ambitious group, and I still remember some of the faces, names, and answers from that night. One young woman, though only seventeen years old, had an incredibly precise view of what she hoped to be her life's work. "I want to go to college, then medical school, and become a pediatric neurosurgeon," she said. None of us sitting there had any doubts that she would become a very successful doctor! Others wanted to be engineers or teachers or lawyers.

There was one young man, extremely bright, who made us all laugh. "I want to be very, very rich," he said. Even though we chuckled, we had every reason to believe that he was utterly serious. He was not pompous or arrogant or conceited. He was simply very clear about his desire to become wealthy. And guess what? He is! A few years ago I ran into a friend in another city, and our conversation somehow unfolded in such a way that this young man's name came up. My friend put it simply: "He is ridiculously wealthy. And also very generous." I was not at all surprised.

The question for most of us isn't whether we'd like to be very rich. The question is whether that is enough. How do we really know what is worth wanting in life? I am quite sure that one could travel to almost any place in the world, including some of the wealthiest neighborhoods in America, and discover that inside any five-mile circle there are hundreds of starving people. In some of those neighborhoods one might find abject poverty and rampant drug abuse. In other neighborhoods one might find incredible wealth and rampant drug abuse. In all those neighborhoods one will find people who are spiritually starved for a life of meaning and purpose, for an existential understanding of what in life is truly important, for the experience of profound love and deep joy. Frankly, who among us has enough of that?

And so here is how I understand this third part of the Lord's Prayer: When Jesus prays "give us this day our daily bread," he is talking about food for those who are physically hungry, but also about much, much more. Jesus is speaking about the spiritual dimension of life, about the quest for love and meaning and hope. He is addressing our deepest needs and greatest longings. He is speaking about giving us *enough*. Enough to be spiritually full as well as physically full.

In the Wilderness

In the sixteenth chapter of the Old Testament book of Exodus we find one of the most important stories in the entire Bible, and it illustrates one of the foundational principles of the life of faith. Moses was leading the Hebrew people through the wilderness to the Promised Land, but they began to panic about whether they would find enough food in that barren and forlorn country. They complained bitterly and wondered aloud why Moses had led them out of Egypt just so they could starve to death:

> *The whole congregation of the Israelites complained against Moses and Aaron in the wilderness. The Israelites said to them, "If only we had died by the hand of the LORD in the land of Egypt, when we sat by the fleshpots and ate our fill of bread; for you have brought us out into this wilderness to kill this whole assembly with hunger."*
>
> (Exodus 16:2-3)

In response to their complaints, God promised the Israelites daily bread that would cover the ground every morning and quail that would fly into their camp every evening to provide all the meat they could consume. There was a caveat, however. They could gather as much manna as they were able to eat each and every morning, but they could not save or store any of it:

> *Then the LORD said to Moses, "I am going to rain bread from heaven for you, and each day the people shall go out and gather enough for that day. In that way I will*

> *test them, whether they will follow my instruction or not."*

> (Exodus 16:4)

When some of the Israelites tried to store and save the bread, worms ruined it by the next morning. God had devised a plan by which the people were forced, literally, to trust God on a daily basis. This is an extraordinarily important story for all Christians.

It is human nature to desire more than enough. Not only do we bolster our sense of security by having more than enough food, wealth, and possessions, but we also want to know more than we need to know about the future. We'd like to wake up each morning and know how things are going to turn out. We'd love to peer into some kind of crystal ball and know that we will arrive at our chosen destinations, that our children will live long and healthy lives, or that the tests the doctor just ran will turn out to be of no concern. We yearn, as did those old Hebrews in the wilderness, for assurances that we and our families are going to be safe and healthy.

But the reality is that, with regard to the really big issues in life, we live in a state of utter insecurity whereby we are totally dependent on God. Think about that for a moment. No matter how much money or possessions one might have, there are absolutely no guarantees when it comes to the most important things in life: our safety and our health, including our mental, emotional, and spiritual health. That truth eludes so many people until they find themselves on the receiving end of bad news. As a pastor I have seen lives turned upside down by one unexpected phone call or one report from the doctor or one split-second bad decision. In fact, I have lived long enough to personally experience this kind of upheaval on more than one occasion. In the long run, no one is exempt.

One of the reasons I remain so committed to the work of the church, including weekly worship, is because of its role in constantly reminding us about the spiritual dimension of everyday life. The day inevitably arrives when our own physical and finite resources of money, status, and power are not enough, and we turn to God and ask for strength and resilience. Those who have remained spiritually tuned to our human limitations and to God's spiritual resources provided on a daily basis are always better equipped to deal with these times of trauma or sadness. To put it succinctly, worship is one of the ways in which we constantly remind ourselves of our human weakness and of God's infinite power and love. It is how we feed ourselves spiritually in order to celebrate abundance in good times and to be prepared to lean upon the grace of God in challenging times. There is no better way to remain faithful and prepared for both the good and bad surprises in life than by worshiping regularly. The good news is that God promises us daily bread—the spiritual, emotional, and mental resources we need—if we will simply trust God one day at a time.

The Bridge

I once had the privilege of working for one of the greatest preachers of his generation. In the early 1970s I attended Perkins School of Theology at Southern Methodist University, and Dr. Robert E. Goodrich hired me to serve on the staff of First United Methodist Church in downtown Dallas. Years earlier my father had served as the senior associate to Dr. Goodrich, and so I had grown up hearing him preach. Working for him was a whole new experience. The brief time I served on Dr. Goodrich's staff before his election as a bishop in the church was one of richest learning experiences of my life.

Through the years I heard Dr. Goodrich preach many memorable sermons, but one in particular left an indelible image in my mind. He preached on Deuteronomy 33:25, which the Revised Standard Version of the Bible translates in this way: "as your days, so is your strength." Dr. Goodrich explicated this verse in a powerful way that is similar to the theme in Exodus 16, emphasizing that our strength comes from our relationship with God, but only one day at a time.

I will never forget how he illustrated that thesis. Imagine, he said, the strongest bridge in the world. Great engineers have given much thought to the design, and the finest contractors have been hired for its construction. It is a structural masterpiece, not only beautiful in design, but built to withstand enormous loads and to last many centuries.

Then, he said, think about the amount of traffic that would cross this bridge in any one day or one week or one year. Automobiles and large trucks and enormous trailers of heavy equipment would be able to cross the bridge with no problem whatsoever as long as they traveled one at a time. As long as the traffic flowed smoothly, the bridge would still be strong and functional even one hundred years later. But what if just one day's traffic were to be placed on the bridge all at once? Even the strongest bridge ever built would crumble under the combined weight of all that traffic.

God created the human being to be like that bridge, he said. If we face our problems and challenges one day at a time, we will always find the strength to endure—as our days, so shall our strength be. But most of us, fallible as we are, are tempted to pile up the weight of many burdens all at once. We will think and worry not just about the challenges awaiting us this day, but also about the failures of the past and the worries of the future. Our sadness about things long gone, and our anxieties about issues we may never actually face, will accelerate our stress about the real issues we are now facing. Like the strongest bridge in the world, not even the strongest person in the world can endure the weight of so many thoughts and worries. No wonder so many of us crumble or fall victim to addiction or to other forms of self-destruction. We simply forget that God gives us the strength to face nearly any crisis, but only one day at a time.

For more than forty years, that image of the bridge has been a reminder to me about the importance of living one day at a time, and of the promise that God will provide enough daily bread—physical, mental, emotional, and spiritual sustenance—to live powerfully even in times of great difficulty.

Matthew 6

If there is any doubt about the importance of living one day at a time as a biblical theme, let's add some verses from the great sixth chapter of Matthew's Gospel. This is a famous and important passage in its own right, well known by those who read and study the Bible on a regular basis. But it has been made even more famous by the hit 1973 musical *Godspell*, which took the passage and turned it into the popular song "Day by Day."

> *Therefore I tell you, do not worry about*
> *your life, what you will eat or what you*
> *will drink, or about your body, what you*
> *will wear. Is not life more than food, and*
> *the body more than clothing? Look at*
> *the birds of the air; they neither sow nor*
> *reap nor gather into barns, and yet your*
> *heavenly Father feeds them. Are you not*
> *of more value than they? And can any of*
> *you by worrying add a single hour to your*
> *span of life? And why do you worry about*

> *clothing? Consider the lilies of the field, how*
> *they grow; they neither toil nor spin, yet I*
> *tell you, even Solomon in all his glory was*
> *not clothed like one of these. But if God so*
> *clothes the grass of the field, which is alive*
> *today and tomorrow is thrown into the*
> *oven, will he not much more clothe you—*
> *you of little faith? Therefore do not worry,*
> *saying, 'What will we eat?' or 'What will we*
> *drink?' or 'What will we wear?' For it is the*
> *Gentiles who strive for all these things; and*
> *indeed your heavenly Father knows that you*
> *need all these things. But strive first for the*
> *kingdom of God and his righteousness, and*
> *all these things will be given to you as well.*
>
> *So do not worry about tomorrow, for*
> *tomorrow will bring worries of its own.*
> *Today's trouble is enough for today.*
>   (Matthew 6:25-34)

I have often said that, if I were stranded on a desert island and could have only one or two chapters of the Bible to read, this would be one of them. These words of Jesus confirm the wisdom of Deuteronomy 33:25 and the great life lessons learned by the Hebrews in Exodus 16. And once we become aware of and sensitized to this important biblical theme, found in both the Old and New Testaments, the words Jesus gave us to pray begin to sound like profound wisdom for our daily journey: "Give us this day our daily bread."

A Big Table

There was a time when I slightly changed this line of the Lord's Prayer every time I prayed it. It was during a very challenging period in my life, and rather than saying "Give *us* our daily bread," I said "Give *me* my daily bread." In my mind this made the prayer more personal as I recounted in the presence of God my need for emotional stability and spiritual confidence while I dealt with some very difficult problems. I have come to believe, however, that Jesus was quite intentional and specific when he instructed the disciples to pray, "Give *us* our daily bread." Jesus was making reference to the distinctly Christian understanding that we do not live alone, we do not suffer alone, and we do not thrive alone. We cannot properly pray for ourselves without praying for others, and when we pray for others we are enriching our own requests for God's presence and grace in our lives.

This thought became even more expansive when I stumbled one day onto a powerful biblical image that I now often use in the praying of this particular line. On numerous occasions in the New Testament, either Jesus is at the table sharing a meal or he tells a parable about a feast or a meal. The most famous meal, of course, was the Last Supper that Jesus shared with his disciples before his crucifixion. In that meal Jesus served as the host, breaking and serving the bread and pouring the wine. He literally fed the disciples.

I like to recreate that scene in my mind as I pray this third part of the Lord's Prayer, but I populate the table with friends and loved ones, and as I meditate on the line "Give us this day our daily bread," I visualize the face of each person at the table and think about the physical, emotional, and spiritual needs of that loved one. I don't pretend to know all those needs, but I trust that God does. This time of focusing on the daily needs of others in that very personal way has become a life-changing discipline for me, helping to mitigate my own tendencies of self-centeredness and narcissism. It has also helped me to feel more empathy for others, some of whom annoy me on occasion. Finally, it has enriched my own very personal requests for spiritual and emotional resources to meet the challenges that lay in front of me.

Let me offer a warning: if you seriously practice this discipline of mentally inviting family and friends to the table where you are sitting and receiving God's grace, it is likely that, in time, others whom you did not invite will show up. In Chapter 5, I'll share with you an experience of praying in this way that presented a genuine spiritual crisis. The daily reciting of the Lord's Prayer eventually led me to a place where I knew that, if I continued, there would be no turning back.

Spiritual Reflection: Receiving God's Daily Bread

One of the most meaningful insights I've received in the past few years is that faith must be practiced on a daily basis if we expect it to be life transforming in any significant way. Once I started paying attention to it, I noticed the call for daily spiritual practice almost everywhere I turned: in the wilderness story of Exodus, in the sixth chapter of Matthew, in the daily routine of Jesus, in the Lord's Prayer, and in the lives of all our saints and role models. It is so obvious! Nothing takes the place of some kind of daily spiritual practice. For this reason, I consider "Give us this day our daily bread" to be the centerpiece of the prayer Jesus taught us. Not only is it placed close to the middle of the prayer, but it is the hinge upon which everything else turns. The very act of saying the prayer is the act of asking God for the physical, emotional, and spiritual sustenance needed for the day.

As I have demonstrated, this particular part of the Lord's Prayer has a rich biblical pedigree, and so this might be the point at which one could be intentional about introducing the reading of Scripture to enrich the spiritual practice. I would offer, again, the sixteenth chapter of Exodus as one of the most important chapters in the Old Testament. It so clearly demonstrates this concept of daily dependence on God, and it does so in the context of the great salvation story that is the experience of the Hebrews as they moved toward the Promised Land. One could, to good advantage, read this story every day for a week or more, committing it firmly to memory in such a way that it is quickly available as a reminder during times of stress. Any period of prayer or meditation preceded by the reading of this story would surely be enriched by its biblical power. The same would be true for the sixth chapter of Matthew, with special emphasis on the closing words of Jesus to strive first for the kingdom of God, allowing today's trouble to be enough for today. And don't forget that little verse from Deuteronomy 33:25.

The Benedictines have a wonderful practice of reading Scripture that is intended to be used with meditation and prayer. Called *Lectio Divina*, it usually involves four separate steps or stages: reading the scripture; meditating on it; praying about it; and contemplating it. John of the Cross put it this way: "Seek in reading and you will find in meditation; knock in prayer and it will be opened to you in contemplation." *Lectio Divina* involves reading Scripture with little dependence on scholarly research or interpretation, but with great reliance on personally experiencing the text. One technique is placing yourself as one of the characters in the biblical story and becoming aware of your emotions and insights. Try using this technique as if Jesus were sitting with you and helping you find personal application in your own life, and the results can be truly eye-opening.

Visualizing this third part of the Lord's Prayer, as I've suggested earlier in this chapter, can make the experience truly sacramental for the person who wants to symbolically formalize the receiving of daily bread. While working on this manuscript, I read David Brooks's wonderful book *The Road to Character* (Random House, 2015), which includes a profile of famed Roman Catholic convert and social worker Dorothy Day. Day converted to Catholicism after living a rather bohemian life in her youth, and in the 1930s she helped establish the Catholic Worker Movement. After her conversion she developed a disciplined lifestyle that included receiving the Holy Eucharist on a daily basis. As Day put it, "After 38 years of almost daily communion, one can confess to a routine, but it is like the routine of taking daily food."[3]

As a lifelong Protestant, the prospect of daily Communion had never occurred to me, and at one time it would have held no appeal. But as a recent convert to spiritual practice, and especially after spending a good deal of time on the concept of daily bread, the symbolic power of the Eucharist has grown in its importance for my spiritual life. I now oftentimes think about the recitation of the Lord's Prayer as a daily receiving of the Eucharist—of God's incarnate presence in the ritual of praying—and I visualize myself at the altar receiving the cup and the bread. I encourage you to experiment with this powerful image as you explore the many ways in which God blesses you with the gifts of daily life.

4

How Can God Forgive Us?

And forgive us our trespasses...

My good friend Bishop Michael McKee tells about being
invited to address a retreat for young people who were soon
to be confirmed as church members. Several hundred boys
and girls were there, most of them in their early teens. Bishop
McKee invited them into conversation, and a thirteen-year-
old boy asked a question that is probably shared by many
people: "How can God forgive me knowing what I've done?"

That's the $64,000 question, isn't it? I don't know about
you, but when I was thirteen I thought I had committed a

lot of sins, and I was worried about it! But I can add up all the sins in the first two decades of my life, and they don't even make a blip on the radar screen today. I suppose that the prevalence of sin should never make us complacent about it, but Paul's reminder to the church in Rome is utterly true: "All have sinned and fall short of the glory of God" (Romans 3: 23).

Indeed, much of Paul's letter to the Romans deals with the ubiquitous nature of sin and the inability of any of us to escape it completely. That's why Paul developed his powerful and lasting theology of grace. *Sola fide* is how Martin Luther put it: we are saved by grace through faith alone! We cannot be redeemed by our good works. That has been a cornerstone of our Christian theology for centuries. Yet, it is a concept that is difficult for us to grasp. Like that young man, at some basic level most of us wonder how God can really forgive all our sins. Reciting the Lord's Prayer on a daily basis is a powerful way of reminding us that not only are we sinners, but that God's forgiveness and grace is freely available to us every single day.

The Original Sin

There is a temptation for us to think of sin solely in terms implied by that young man in Bishop McKee's audience. We think of the constant daily temptations or sins of the flesh. It is helpful and important for us to understand that, in the eyes of God, sin is both more subtle and more prevalent than that. The great Christian writer and apologist

C. S. Lewis once wrote, "The sins of the flesh are bad, but they are the least bad of all sins. All the worst pleasures are purely spiritual: the pleasure of putting other people in the wrong, of bossing and patronizing and spoiling sport, and back-biting; the pleasures of power, of hatred."[4] Those words are an important reminder to examine the root cause of all sin, the story of which can be found in the familiar story of Genesis:

> *Now the serpent was more crafty than any*
> *other wild animal that the LORD God had*
> *made. He said to the woman, "Did God*
> *say, 'You shall not eat from any tree in the*
> *garden'?" The woman said to the serpent,*
> *"We may eat of the fruit of the trees in the*
> *garden; but God said, 'You shall not eat*
> *of the fruit of the tree that is in the middle*
> *of the garden, nor shall you touch it, or*
> *you shall die.' " But the serpent said to the*
> *woman, "You will not die; for God knows*
> *that when you eat of it your eyes will be*
> *opened, and you will be like God, knowing*
> *good and evil." So when the woman saw that*
> *the tree was good for food, and that it was a*
> *delight to the eyes, and that the tree was to*
> *be desired to make one wise, she took of its*
> *fruit and ate; and she also gave some to her*
> *husband, who was with her, and he ate.*
>
> (Genesis 3:1-6)

It is important to note that the Bible starts with the drama of creation, and it is a drama about perfection. In the climactic moment of the creative process, God creates the human "in the image" of God. The first chapter closes with these words: "God saw everything that he had made, and indeed, it was very good" (Genesis 1:31). The fact that God's creation is unambiguously good is foundational to our Christian understanding of the universe.

But the story moves from the drama of perfection to the drama of sin, and it is important for us to pay close attention to how this happens. Since the beginning of time humans have wrestled with the issue of sin. This ancient text, so easily discarded by modern Christians as mere mythology or symbolism, still provides provocative insights into the sinful nature of the human being. When examined closely, the story of the Fall includes one of the most extraordinary insights into the nature of the human being ever written.

So what happened? Pay careful attention to the drama that was unfolding in the garden. Since the humans were made in God's image, the man and woman had the freedom to choose, and God placed only one restriction on them: do not eat of the tree of knowledge. Everything else was freely theirs. Now note the serpent's words when he tells the woman of the forbidden tree: "You will not die; for God knows that when you eat of it your eyes will be opened, and you will be like God" (Genesis 3:4).

You will be like God! That was the temptation, and it was impossible to resist. The desire to be like God—it was the temptation of pride, the desire to be all-powerful and all-knowing.

Much later, in the brilliant second chapter of his letter to the Philippians, Paul described how Christ reversed the "original sin" by making the opposite choice from the one made by Adam and Eve:

> *Let the same mind be in you that was in*
> *Christ Jesus,*
>
> > *who, though he was in the form of God,*
> > *did not regard equality with God*
> > *as something to be exploited,*
> > *but emptied himself,*
> > *taking the form of a slave,*
> > *being born in human likeness.*
> > *And being found in human form,*
> > *he humbled himself*
> > *and became obedient to the point*
> > *of death—*
> > *even death on a cross.*
>
> (Philippians 2:5-8)

It is clear that Paul considered pride, or the desire to be like God, to be the "original sin," and it was this sin that was "reversed" in Jesus' decision to be fully human by going to the cross.

Paul once wrote one of the most poignant passages in the Bible. In what can only be described as a frustrated outcry, he penned, "I do not understand my own actions. For I do not do what I want, but I do the very thing I hate" (Romans 7:15). Who cannot identify with Paul's plight? But, in truth, Paul did understand the source of his sin. It was the inevitable temptation of pride, the desire to be *like* God rather than to be *obedient* to God. That is what drives our ongoing choices that are inconsistent with God's will for us. It is our pride and our narcissism that lead us to what the theologian Paul Tillich called our "separation from God." And Paul knew that the only answer to sin is not law or legal requirements, but rather *re*-union with God through confession, forgiveness, and the magnificent acceptance that comes through God's grace. Praying the Lord's Prayer on a daily basis is a way of reminding ourselves that not only are we sinners, but that God has the power and the desire to forgive us and restore us to wholeness.

God Forgives and Forgets

The most remarkable aspect of our grace-filled theology is that God not only forgives our sins but forgets them as well. The writer of Hebrews pens a remarkable statement in the eighth chapter:

> *"This is the covenant that I will make with*
> *the house of Israel*
> *   after those days, says the Lord:*
> *I will put my laws in their minds,*
> *   and write them on their hearts,*
> *and I will be their God,*

> *and they shall be my people.*
> *And they shall not teach one another*
> *or say to each other, 'Know the Lord,'*
> *for they shall all know me,*
> *from the least of them to the greatest.*
> *For I will be merciful toward their iniquities,*
> *and I will remember their sins no more."*
>
> (Hebrews 8:10-12)

I will remember their sins no more! How could this be true? We humans have the ability to remember forever the slightest insult or smallest betrayal. We often hold on to grudges as if they are among our most valuable possessions. We are acutely aware of every transgression into our personal space. If someone's words or actions are ambiguous, we often attribute the worst possible interpretation. No wonder we have trouble with forgiveness! If we can't forgive others (we're getting to that part later), how can we forgive ourselves? And how can we expect God to forgive us?

The promise that God will remember our sins no more is such a remarkable expression of God's grace that we have trouble actually believing it. If we could live on a daily basis with perfect trust in that promise, we would live extraordinary and graceful and joyful lives. But forgiving and forgetting is such a challenge for us personally that this news is hard to assimilate. And, frankly, one of the biggest obstacles to living freely in the kingdom of God is not what God remembers about us, but what we remember about ourselves. The memories we carry with us are so powerful that they can keep us chained to the past. Reciting the Lord's Prayer on a daily basis is one of the ways we retrain our minds and spirits to be receptive to the grace and love of a forgiving God. We need to hear the prayer over and over until it becomes our dominant way of thinking.

The Power of Memory

At the age of thirty-five I decided to take up the game of golf. That may have been a bad decision in itself, but it was followed by an even worse one. I convinced myself that if I read some books, watched some videotapes, and studied the professionals on television, I could teach myself how to play. Several frustrating years later I employed a professional to help me. He asked me to swing a few times, which I did. "That's the worse golf swing I've ever seen," he said. He then added, "I have good news and bad news for you. The good news is that it is possible to fix that swing. The bad news is that it will be very, very difficult." He then proceeded to deliver a lecture on muscle memory, and how I had trained my muscles all those years to remember that bad swing. The only way to fix it would be to swing correctly so many times that my muscles would lose their memory of the old swing.

Memory is a powerful thing, isn't it? Not only powerful, but essential. Without memory a person would never be able to find their car in the parking lot or develop ongoing relationships with loved ones. Most of us have witnessed, either personally or in the lives of friends or loved ones, the devastating effects of Alzheimer's disease or severe dementia. We sometimes speak jokingly about losing our memory, but we know it is no laughing matter. Truthfully, the stress of everyday life places enough demands on our memory that most of us, even the young, sometimes struggle with the challenges of remembering things we consider to be important.

But memory can also have a demonic and destructive dimension that we often don't discuss. It occurs, oddly enough, when we are unable to *forget* something. Sometimes we carry around painful or scary memories that will not turn us loose. When we cannot get rid of bad or painful thoughts from our past, our memory can nearly destroy us.

In a scene from Larry McMurtry's novel *Texasville*, a sequel to his well-known book *The Last Picture Show*, Duane looks for his friend Sonny, who has gone missing. Sonny has been acting strangely for some time, "losing it" as we are prone to say, and his friends are worried. Duane finally finds Sonny in their town's dilapidated movie theater, sitting with a blank look on his face and "playing reruns in his head." It is a poignant moment and a scene that I have remembered for many years. The reason? Many of us are like Sonny, compulsively playing reruns in our heads of old mistakes and failures and sins. When that compulsiveness becomes extreme, we can literally become ill because our memory has imprisoned us in a world of angst and grief and failure. When we can't get the past out of our head, when we keep playing mental reruns of everything that has gone wrong in life, we are flirting with mental, emotional, and spiritual dysfunction.

Paul pens a memorable phrase in his letter to the Philippians. In the third chapter he writes,

> *Beloved, I do not consider that I have made*
> *it my own; but this one thing I do: forgetting*
> *what lies behind and straining forward to*
> *what lies ahead, I press on toward the goal*
> *for the prize of the heavenly call of God in*
> *Christ Jesus.*

(Philippians 3:13-14)

Forgetting what lies behind! He is speaking very personally, and one cannot help but wonder about the memories Paul is trying to let go of. Do you suppose he was haunted by the memory of those days when he was a pure legalist, following the law to the minutest detail and yet still unhappy and frustrated? Did he keep seeing himself as the arrogant, pompous, self-righteous Pharisee he had been before he met Christ? Was it that moment when he held the coats of those who stoned Stephen? Paul brought a lot of baggage to his relationship with Christ, and in this remarkable moment of self-revelation we glimpse his struggles to stop playing those old reruns in his head.

We know what those reruns are like, don't we? From the former athlete who dropped the pass in the championship game, to the person who committed a sin or made a mistake long ago, our memories of the past can imprison us for life if we are not careful. Some, like Paul himself, live with horrific memories of terrible choices or tragic accidents. And so Paul writes these memorable four words in his letter to the Philippians: "forgetting what lies behind."

When we pray "forgive us our trespasses" in the Lord's Prayer, we are trusting God not only to forgive us but also to provide us with the spiritual power to accept that forgiveness. We are giving our sins to God, but we are also asking for God's power and grace to help us stop playing the reruns in our heads. Many people know and understand that God forgives, but they are still not liberated by grace. The reason is the demonic power of memory.

Stages of Forgiveness

In order for this phrase of the Lord's Prayer to be fully liberating, there is a sequence that must be fully experienced. The first stage in this sequence is trusting that God does indeed forgive us. It means accepting that God's forgiveness is not superficial or temporary but sincere and lasting. The second stage is trusting that God forgets, that God remembers our sins no more. This stage is difficult because of our human tendency to remember the smallest of infractions, our compulsive desire to hold on to painful memories. How can we understand that what is unnatural for us is natural for God? The final and most difficult stage is the forgetting that we ourselves must do. The glory of a full relationship with

Christ is found when believers become so confident about God's love that they are liberated from dwelling on all that has gone wrong.

You may be thinking that practiced amnesia is not particularly virtuous or helpful for a person striving to become a better human being. After all, most of us grew up hearing the admonition to "learn from your mistakes." Paul penned "forgetting what lies behind," but he clearly did not forget the sins of commission and omission from his youth, or he would not have written about them when teaching his people. In fact, he co-opted those memories and used them to become wiser and more insightful.

Paul provides a model for how to deal with our own struggles. Paul could and did recall his past mistakes, but he was not obsessed by them. One might say that God's grace had liberated him from the shame of his failures. They no longer held emotional power over him. In fact, he seems to have experienced a certain element of joy in their recollection, for the simple reason that he knew and fully accepted that he had been forgiven and redeemed.

There are prayer cards in the pews of our church in Plano, Texas, and every Sunday people fill them out and drop them in the plates. Most of the time the cards are submitted anonymously, and they are read out loud in our staff meetings on the following Wednesday as we support our members and visitors with our prayers. Many years ago there was a prayer request—actually a prayer joy—that I will never forget: "Thanks for my two sons who have forgiven me for being an imperfect father." As the father of two sons, I have voiced a similar prayer on many occasions. When you examine closely this prayer of thanks, it includes the memory of being an imperfect father, but it also expresses the joy of being forgiven. In fact, the joy of being forgiven clearly overcomes the regret and pain of all that had gone wrong. This man no longer obsesses over past mistakes and is no longer held by the power of regret or shame. Instead, he celebrates the loving relationships made possible by true forgiveness. I think that is what happened with Paul, and it is a model of what it means to truly accept the forgiveness that is so freely offered by God.

Jubilee

A friend and church member is a Latin teacher in a very fine Roman Catholic high school. Several years ago, after hearing me preach on the Lord's Prayer, she shared with me a delightful insight:

> During the first quarter of school, I pray the Pater Noster ["Our Father"] with my students at the start of every class, and I require my Latin students to memorize it. The daily time we spend with it allows me to explore new facets of it year after year. My realization this year? When talking about "trespasses" in the English, the word is *debita* in the Latin, which means "those things owed." Literally, that section is "forgive us for the things we owe you, just like we forgive

those people owing us something." The kids are often moved to realize that it isn't just about sins, but also about other kinds of obligations and debts. Then, it allows me to discuss what a Jubilee year is all about. What an amazing thing to be able to ask God for the privilege of always living in a communal state of Jubilee!"*

My friend is referring to an Old Testament Hebrew tradition that is not well known by many Christians. Known as the year of Jubilee, it called for the forgiveness of all debts every fifty years, including the return of slaves to their original families. The commandment for Jubilee is found in the book of Leviticus:

> *And you shall hallow the fiftieth year and you shall proclaim liberty throughout the land to all its inhabitants. It shall be a jubilee for you: you shall return, every one of you, to your property and every one of you to your family.*

(Leviticus 25:10)

This ancient tradition is no longer practiced, even in the Jewish community. But the concept of Jubilee offers a unique insight into the meaning of the Lord's Prayer. As in other parts of the prayer, the emphasis is communal as well as

---

* Given the Latin word and its definition, it's easy to see why in some traditions the words *debts* and *debtors* are used in the Lord's Prayer. There are subtle distinctions between *trespasses* and *debts*, but for our purposes we will treat the terms as interchangeable.

personal. When instructing the disciples how to pray, Jesus doesn't say, "Forgive *my* trespasses." Rather, he is consistent in using plural pronouns throughout the prayer, reflecting the Jewish emphasis on the life of the individual as part of a community. As discussed in the chapter about daily bread, a person cannot fully enjoy the benefits of God's abundance as a solitary experience. In order to claim the magnificence of God's bounty, it must be what I call a "solidarity" experience rather than a solitary experience. One person is not fed unless all are fed. One person is not free unless all are free. One person cannot live in the fullness of God's forgiveness and grace without embracing the power of grace for all persons. The vision that Jesus gives us in the Lord's Prayer is, in fact, a vision of Jubilee: all people forgiven, fed, and liberated. It is nothing less than the kingdom of God on earth as it is in heaven.

Of course, this point in the prayer is where things become truly difficult. It is one thing to ask forgiveness for ourselves; it is another to forgive those who have hurt us. If we return to Paul's statement from Philippians about "forgetting what lies behind," the challenge to forget our own failures can seem like child's play when compared with the task of forgiving and forgetting those who have hurt us.

Spiritual Reflection: Embracing Mercy

When I first began including meditation as a form of daily spiritual practice, I quickly discovered that one of the greatest challenges involves controlling the flow of my own thoughts. Since meditation literally forces a person to slow down—to step back from the chaos of everyday life—it can sometimes invite the mind into even greater activity. At its most effective, meditation slows the human being down to one second at a time, or at least one breath at a time, with the goal of living fully in that moment. However, almost anyone who begins to experiment with meditation will discover that retreating from the frantic activity that consumes our waking hours will initially produce the opposite result. Liberated from the tasks of daily work or raising a family, the mind will inevitably begin to wander forward or backward in time. The forward motion of the mind will have one thinking about the tasks of the day or the challenges posed by some looming event. The backward motion of the mind will find a person obsessing about something that went wrong in the past, a transgression committed or an injury received. It is at this point, I believe, that many people give up on the practice. What is the point of all this silence if it simply reinforces negative or stressful thoughts? What is the point of asking for God's forgiveness if, in the midst of this spiritual practice, I find myself playing those old scenes over and over?

I have come to believe that one of the best ways of understanding spiritual practice is by analogy to physical practice. When a person makes a commitment to more robust health by starting a routine of jogging or biking or weightlifting, they know from the beginning that the initial results aren't going to feel entirely good. The production of lactic acid will increase, muscles will fatigue, and soreness will follow. Initial workouts, no matter how simple or short, will be challenging, and the first week or two may result in a feeling of decreased energy and increased discomfort. Seasoned athletes understand that this initial experience is simply the price one pays for the long-term benefits of fitness, health, and vitality. They might even embrace an attitude of "short-term pain equals long-term gain," celebrating the sore muscles and discomfort as a sign that they are "on track" to reap the positive benefits of working out.

Spiritual practice is not dissimilar. Believing that one week of twenty-minute meditation sessions will produce a mystical guru is as delusional as believing that one week of jogging will yield the physical capacity to run a marathon. The "gains" one experiences in daily spiritual practice are mostly incremental, with the occasional recognition that one has reached a new level of awareness or inner peacefulness. It should also be acknowledged that, just as with physical injuries for the athlete, there can be setbacks that are prompted by unusual stress or particularly challenging circumstances. Those are the times when commitment to the practice needs to be reaffirmed.

This pattern of setbacks and stress, persistence and breakthroughs, certainly has been true for me personally. I suspect it's true for most people with regard to fully accepting the gift of God's mercy and forgiveness. At the intellectual level, and perhaps even spiritually, it is not hard to understand and fully accept God's forgiveness and mercy. It is the psychic challenge—the obsessive wandering of the mind—that holds us back. We tend to remember reflexively the bad things we've done, along with all those stupid and embarrassing moments. Our minds are tenacious: they love to hold on! But over time, if we permit those thoughts to arrive but then allow them to leave by focusing on God's mercy in the moment, we will find that our psychic muscles will begin to catch up with our spiritual muscles. It may take weeks or months, but over time the reruns in our head will be replaced by the vital awareness that God remembers no more, and neither should we.

5

The Unforgiven

…as we forgive those who trespass against us.

A number of years ago I was talking with a friend who is a highly successful businessman. The conversation turned to an associate of his with whom I had experienced a very negative encounter many years earlier. His associate had done nothing illegal or immoral, but he had been rude and cavalier about a request to help out my church in a very simple way. I shared with my friend how much I resented the attitude of his colleague and the words he had spoken to me twenty-five years earlier. My friend's response was simple and unequivocal: "You need to put that behind you."

Even as he spoke those words I recalled that I was listening to a person who had been hurt tremendously by his association with a minor scandal many years earlier. He had been unfairly savaged by the media and by rumors, both private and public. It had almost destroyed his career. If there was ever a person who had reason to hold on to resentment and grudges, it would be him. And yet, he had clearly "put it behind him" and rebuilt a solid career and a joyful life. When he told me to let it go, I understood that I was listening to the profound wisdom of a person who clearly understood how the refusal to forgive others can become deeply destructive. I have never forgotten the lesson of that conversation, and I knew that I was hearing in his words the voice of Jesus.

Paying Attention

When I first started being more thoughtful about the Lord's Prayer, I decided to slow down my recital of it and to pay close attention to each phrase. This was about the same time that I began to practice contemplation, and I had tasted the benefits of slowing down and "staying in the moment." I soon discovered that the way in which I prayed the Lord's Prayer—the pacing, the pauses, the moments of emphasis—was uneven and prejudicial. It revealed my own biases and weaknesses. Indeed, it revealed my own pride and narcissism.

For instance, I discovered that I slowed down when I got to the phrase "Give us this day our daily bread." I found myself lingering over that phrase and investing a good deal of time and emotional energy in it, especially if I was experiencing stress. I'm not sure lingering over it was a bad thing. That phrase is located near the middle of the prayer, and, as I have stated earlier, it reflects an extraordinary and important biblical theme. The importance of being fed—physically, mentally, emotionally, and spiritually—really does lie at the center of the prayer in many ways. Unless we become recipients of God's daily manna, we really aren't capable of living out the rest of the prayer. But there were times when I prayed the Lord's Prayer as if that one phrase were the only truly important part. And I soon learned that my attentiveness to that phrase was leading to disregard of other parts of the prayer.

The second phrase I often spent some time on was the one immediately following: "Forgive us our trespasses." It doesn't require a highly sensitive conscience to be aware of one's mistakes and failures. Like that young teenager in Bishop McKee's audience, I know I'm a sinner. At my best, I hunger for God's forgiveness and for a new start. I relish God's forgetfulness. I cling to the power of redemption. The sheer knowledge that Jesus taught us to pray "forgive us our trespasses" instills confidence and hope that we can celebrate lives that have been liberated from the weight of the past. It would not come as a surprise to me to learn that these two phrases command the emotional attention of most people who pray the Lord's Prayer. They certainly did for me.

That leads us, of course, to that moment when I had to confront the difficult second part of the statement Jesus gave us. He didn't just say, "Forgive us our trespasses." The full statement is "Forgive us our trespasses, *as* we forgive those who trespass against us." I intentionally place emphasis on the word *as* to demonstrate what I think Jesus intended: our liberation from the sins we have committed goes hand-in-hand with our own graciousness towards those who have hurt us. Notice that I said "hand-in-hand." I do not believe Jesus was saying that it is cause and effect, that if we forgive others God will forgive us. Rather, Jesus was making the point that we really are unable to fully receive the grace God offers freely unless we are willing to offer it as well.

I have thought about this part of the prayer a great deal, and I think it is unambiguous. At a superficial or strictly cognitive level, we can know and understand that God forgives us our sins without struggling with the commandment for us to forgive others. But at the emotional and spiritual depths, it is impossible to accept completely the opportunity to live in the power and freedom of God's amazing grace until we have offered the same for those who have trespassed against us.

We should pause here to ponder the importance and gravity of that statement. It is not particularly good news for those of us who, through the years, have blithely assumed God's mercy in our own lives without taking seriously the reciprocity demanded of us. In fact, the well-known words *cheap grace* may refer as much to this self-centered understanding of God's grace as it does to our tendency to ask for forgiveness without mending our ways. And yet, if we will fully trust the prayer Jesus gave us, and go all the way in praying it and living it, we might find surprising benefits for our spiritual and emotional lives.

The Challenge

The challenge lies in the fact that we cherish our bitter memories and grudges, the old tales of how someone belittled us or undermined us or hurt us deeply. We love replaying them in our mind, compulsively reliving the feelings of contempt and disregard—might we even say hatred?—for those who in some way have wronged us. We possess fertile imaginations that are capable of sprouting ever-new scenarios of how we might get even, or how our transgressors might eventually receive their just rewards. And this tendency to replay the drama of our pain can be self-reinforcing. The more we think about it, the worse it becomes. Sometimes we can even imagine, with great righteous indignation, the ways in which others have been hurt by our enemies. The sides are drawn, and we stand with goodness and truth while our opponents represent evil of the worst kind.

If I appear to be hyperbolic or facetious on this point, let me quickly acknowledge that when it comes to "those who trespass against us," there are many different kinds of reality represented by that phrase. A few years ago I was having a quiet lunch in a small town café when an older gentleman started complaining loudly to a group of friends who had gathered at his table. I wasn't intentionally eavesdropping, but this man was talking so loudly that everyone in the room could hear him. In a long, rambling rant about his "Mama," he recounted how years earlier his mother had evidently made a minor decision that favored one of his siblings, and how bitter he was about it. This man was easily in his seventies, his mother was long dead, and yet he was still so possessed of anger and jealousy that he was making a fool of himself in front of his friends. Evidently he could neither forgive nor forget this incident, even though it was in fact merely a small blip on the big radar screen of his life. It was a perfect demonstration of a reality I have often observed and have often been guilty of: We love the idea of God having a short memory when it comes to *our* sins, but we have elephant memories when it comes to the sins of those who have hurt us. We *enjoy* remembering the transgressions of those who have somehow offended us or made us angry!

On the other hand, there are those who have been hurt so deeply that any kind of superficial discussion of forgiveness is insulting and cavalier. Many years ago, as a young pastor, I preached a sermon on forgiving our enemies in which I articulated that challenge as a kind of routine requirement of Christians. I didn't say it was easy, but neither did I acknowledge how terribly difficult it can be. A friend later challenged me by saying, "Your problem, Don, is that you've never been a victim." As I thought about it, she was right.

I had never been truly hurt or victimized in some deeply painful way.

Not long after that, a church member came to counsel with me, and shared the long-held and deeply painful childhood memory of being sexually abused by a parent. From that moment on, my perspective has been considerably broadened. In the ensuing years, I have preached about the importance of forgiveness on many occasions, but never once without reminding myself that in the congregation there were undoubtedly those who had been sinned against in unthinkable ways. In fact, I will often acknowledge to the congregation that "some of you have been hurt in ways I can't imagine."

Some readers, in this moment, will be reliving yet again the trauma of being victimized, perhaps many years ago. For others who perhaps have never truly been victims, it is my hope that this section will be a reminder that some of the people around you have experienced unseen and unspoken pain that has formed them in ways you might not completely understand. And surely it will be an opportunity to reflect in new ways and with a new perspective on those persons and events in your own life that have been difficult for you to forgive.

Releasing Burdens

Having acknowledged the difficulty of the task posed by this part of the prayer, it must be said that nothing can destroy a person's life faster than holding on to grievances and painful memories. The emotional and spiritual price of not confronting the challenge of forgiving one's enemies is simply greater than most of us can bear, and the consequences are often seen in depression, addiction, compulsive anxiety, and other afflictions. The offices of psychotherapists around the world are filled with people who are still struggling to come to terms with old hurts and those who inflicted them.

Many years ago a colleague of mine provided an extraordinary and thoughtful articulation of our need to offer forgiveness, especially for those we are closest to. He said there is no worse burden to live with than a mother or father no longer alive, but not yet forgiven, and that it is precisely what cannot be *condoned* that *must* be *forgiven*.

There are three words in the statement that I think are pivotal, so I've placed them in italics. It is extraordinarily important to recognize the difference between forgiving and condoning. Note that "...what cannot be condoned" is an unequivocal statement. There are many transgressions that under no circumstances can or should be condoned. It is my belief that when a person struggles with the issue of forgiveness, they easily confuse these two concepts. In the midst of the anger or pain or sadness of remembering the events associated with some kind of harm done to them, it is easy to react internally with a "No! No! No! I cannot forgive such a horrible thing." If one can move to saying, "No! No! No! I will never *condone* such a horrible thing," it is then possible to move to the next stage of forgiveness—which is not the same thing.

Forgiving what cannot be condoned is required for the process of healing. It is a bitter and ironic truth that the inability to forgive enables the perpetrator to continue his or her victimization into perpetuity. In the final analysis, the decision to forgive (but not condone) is often mostly made in the self-interest of the victim rather than the perpetrator. It is one of the ways in which a person can say about a person or event out of her past, "I'm not going to allow you to hurt me anymore. I will never condone what happened. But I will no longer be captive to these painful memories or to the hatred that has sapped so much of my emotional energy and my hope for the future. I know that you, too, are a wounded child of God. I do not condone what happened, but I forgive you, even as I have been forgiven, and I plea for the grace of God to allow me to begin the process of also forgetting."

I am not going to claim that forgiving others is easy. I do not believe that most people can read this chapter and, in an inspired moment, simply forgive and forget. In fact, where there has been great harm done, I believe that it requires ongoing spiritual work, often accompanied by help from a qualified therapist. Most of us could use that kind of help from time to time when dealing with even less traumatic events in our lives. A well-trained and gifted spiritual director or therapist can play an important role in mediating the journey toward forgiveness and healing.

I also believe that consistently praying the Lord's Prayer, with intentionality and thoughtfulness about the power of forgiveness, both received and given, can play a large role in that journey. Like every enormous challenge, progress can be made one day at a time until the moment comes when suddenly there is a major breakthrough. It may not be total or lasting forgiveness, but it will be enough to know that the journey is worth it, that progress can continue, and that healing, wholeness, and joy are the destination.

The Three Dimensions of Time

As we approach the close of these two chapters on forgiveness, there is a compelling, overarching question that must be confronted by the person who prays the Lord's Prayer: Will I live my life this day in a way that is burdened and haunted by the past, or will I live a liberated and joyous life that is empowered by God's promise of a grace-filled future? This question articulates the existential choice each person makes every single day, either consciously or unconsciously. Praying the Lord's Prayer on a daily basis can be perhaps the single most powerful discipline in our commitment to live a joyous life of faith, commitment, and love.

Once again, the story of the Hebrew people wandering in the wilderness may best illustrate this quandary of faith in their struggle with the three dimensions of time: past, present, and future. The intention of God for the Hebrews was unambiguous. It was God's desire for the people to be motivated by the vision of the Promised Land, liberated from the slavery of the past, and utterly committed to living joyously and faithfully in the present moment by trusting fully in God. The drama of the manna appearing daily, discussed in Chapter 3, is one of the most important stories in the Old Testament. It clearly teaches about God's desire for us to stay "in the moment" and to resist the anxiety of obsessing about either the past or the future.

All three dimensions of time—past, present, and future—are important, but properly defining and assimilating the role of these dimensions is essential. God desires for us to remember the past to the extent that it provides a foundation for learning and wisdom. But God wants us to forget and let go of the past when it holds us emotionally captive to painful memories, or when it tempts us to return to old ways of living. Remember, there was a moment when the Hebrews were so anxious about having enough food that they longed to return to slavery in Egypt. This is not their story alone, but rather a compelling biblical paradigm of how we all can be seduced by memories of the past and by our longing for security rather than freedom, for certainty rather than faith.

Occasionally someone will ask me to interpret the Revelation of John, the last book of the Bible. It is a complex book, composed in a style known as Jewish apocalyptic literature, and it is full of intricate and picturesque symbolism. My standard three-minute commentary is that the book remains a mystery to me for the most part, but that I understand its primary message to be a vision of God's intended future for us. Ultimately, it paints an unforgettable image of God's closing chapter of history:

> *See, the home of God is among mortals.*
> *He will dwell with them;*
> *they will be his peoples,*
> *and God himself will be with them;*
> *he will wipe every tear from their eyes.*
> *Death will be no more;*
> *mourning and crying and pain will be no more,*
> *for the first things have passed away.*
>
> (Revelation 21:3-4)

For Christians, the vision in Revelation is the promised land God is calling us to. It is intended to inspire in us confidence in God's ultimate plan and to motivate us to stay on the journey. We are always invited and encouraged to remember the past for instruction and wisdom, but the trajectory of our lives should always be forward, future-oriented, and hopeful. And yet, God calls us to *live* the journey faithfully by staying in the moment and experiencing each day in a trusting relationship with the One who provides and sustains us with all we need for that day.

Whose Table Is It?

In Chapter 3, I described my experience of praying "Give us this day our daily bread" while visualizing the faces of friends and loved ones seated at the table. I found the practice to be comforting and enriching, and it helped me feel less self-centered and more empathetic.

Then one morning, as I went around the table, I suddenly found myself gazing upon the face of someone whom I had not invited! Not only was this person not invited, but I was not inclined to show any welcome. I stated earlier in this chapter that I have never really been a victim, but this cannot be said about some of the people I care about. Sitting in front of me, surrounded by family and friends who were sharing the table, was a person whom I deeply resented. I had, in recent years, spent hour upon hour recalling the ways in which this person had hurt someone who is very dear to me. And I had spent an equal number of hours fantasizing about the ways in which I might even the score or see this person receive a "just reward."

It was a moment of utter spiritual crisis for me. I confess that my reflexive inclination was to turn the table over on this person. I was confused to the point of bewilderment. My "family dinner table" had been invaded by one of the last people in the world I would invite. This person was sitting an arm's length from the loved one who had been so terribly hurt. The quiet peacefulness of my meditation had been not just interrupted by this invader; it had been shattered.

It was at this point in my spiritual journey that I had to deal with a very challenging question: Was this my table or the Lord's table? I had adopted the visual practice from stories in the New Testament in which Jesus was clearly presiding at the table, but in typical self-centered fashion I had gradually usurped the role of host. It had become *my* table, populated by *my* guests, and I had silently claimed the authority to determine who was and was not welcome.

As I pondered this self-inflicted dilemma, I looked down the table and found myself staring into the gentle face of yet another person. Silently gazing upon me with a look of incredible kindness was none other than Jesus. Without actually speaking the words, he conveyed an unambiguous message: "Whose table is it? You decide."

As I struggled with that question, two things became clear to me. The first was that this meaningful practice of sitting with others and asking for daily bread would lose all its spiritual power if I claimed the table for myself. The table would have to be the Lord's, or it would have to go away. Angry as I was, my rational mind could reach no other conclusion. The second was the realization that if I continued with this spiritual practice, I would have to deal with the very messy issue of forgiveness in ways that would be far more profound and troubling than I had ever imagined. I knew that Jesus would continue to invite people to the table who would make me angry or uncomfortable. I also knew this was by design. I came to understand that when Jesus instructed us to forgive those who have trespassed against us, he was dead serious about the commandment. If I decided to remain at the Lord's table, there would be no turning back.

As the table has grown larger over time, and I have experienced the healing and wholeness that can come only with forgiveness, I have begun to appreciate more fully the profound depth of God's love. It is relatively easy to stand in the pulpit and utter generalizations about God's love or witness to a friend about the grace of God. Most of the time we are thinking of ourselves when we speak about that kind of love. Being forced to consider God's love and grace for someone we have despised, however, eventually leads us to a much deeper understanding of our own brokenness and of the depth and breadth of God's love for us all. Saying the Lord's Prayer on a daily basis had led me to a spiritual place I could never have imagined.

Spiritual Reflection: Living Without Anger or Blame

I confess that it is somewhat jolting for me every time I read this particular chapter. Though for years I have told personal stories in my sermons, the degree of confession and personal candor in the chapter goes beyond anything I typically would have shared. Like spiritual practice itself, this book has propelled me into territory I did not intend. I am hopeful readers will understand that these insights and experiences are poured from a terribly flawed vessel and certainly not from a mature or seasoned spirituality. Maybe that fact alone will provide encouragement to readers who believe they are not yet ready for a commitment to spiritual practice.

Having entered my fifth decade of ministry, after hearing stories told by hundreds of people through the years, it is my strong belief that there is no road to healing, wholeness, and joy that does not confront the painful challenges involved in accepting and offering forgiveness. I suspect that most psychotherapists would agree. At the root of nearly all our anger, depression, anxiety, and guilt are the unreconciled memories of the sins we have committed or the injuries we have received. Ironically, our own guilt is often intertwined with our anger toward those who have hurt us, and we find it difficult to extricate ourselves from this vicious cycle. Unable to receive mercy and fully forgive ourselves, we are unwilling to offer mercy and forgiveness to others, thus producing anger and frustration that tighten the grip of painful memories.

I honestly believe that, for many people, spiritual practice is the only way to become liberated from this death spiral of unreconciled grievances. We can intellectually understand God's free grace and fully accept the need to forgive others as we have been forgiven, and yet still remain trapped in an emotional prison that has been constructed of anger and blame. Spiritual practice, defined simply as allowing God to be present to a person through prolonged periods of silence, may be the most powerful way to accept the gift of mercy for oneself, thereby opening the door for offering mercy to others.

It is my belief that unless one has fully accepted God's mercy for oneself, the project of trying to fully forgive others is a fool's errand. Thus, communion with God becomes the beginning, the centerpiece, and the anchor of a life that has been liberated in all directions by the gift of forgiveness. These two chapters on forgiveness, therefore, are intricately tied to one another, and it is easy to see why Jesus said to pray like this: "Forgive us our trespasses, as we forgive those who trespass against us." Jesus knew that wholeness begins with receiving God's grace, but that it is not complete until such grace has been extended to others.

6

Tempted by What?

And lead us not into temptation,
but deliver us from evil.

"Does God really tempt us?" she asked.

I had just finished my final sermon in a series on the Lord's Prayer, and I had mostly skipped discussion of the phrase "lead us not into temptation." That was partly due to timing constraints, but as I look back I must confess it was also because of the question just posed by the worshiper. To be honest, at that time I had neither the time nor the desire to flesh out the rather daunting conclusion of the prayer Jesus taught us. But her question was a fair one, and inevitable.

What are we saying when we ask God not to lead us into temptation?

"Lead us not into temptation" is in some ways the most challenging line in the Lord's Prayer. When read literally, it is inconsistent with other biblical references to temptation. For instance, we know that Jesus himself was tempted in the wilderness. The Letter of James opens with a discussion of how "the testing of your faith produces endurance" (James 1:3). Then James proceeds to address the question head-on: "No one, when tempted, should say, 'I am being tempted by God'; for God cannot be tempted by evil and he himself tempts no one. But one is tempted by one's own desire, being lured and enticed by it" (James 1:13-14).

New Testament scholar Douglas Hare, to whom I am indebted for some of the above insights, takes a helpful and pragmatic approach to this issue: "It is probable, therefore, that the way most Christians have understood this petition, while in tension with its surface meaning, is nonetheless correct: 'Grant me the strength to resist temptation.'"[5] Dr. Hare goes on to suggest that the phrase "deliver us from evil" (which is not present in Luke's version of the prayer) is probably Matthew's attempt to bring more clarity to the temptation phrase. For the purposes of this discussion, we will consider the two phrases in precisely this way: together, they form a powerful petition for divine guidance and help in avoiding the evil deeds that are often the consequences of our temptations.

Pride

Moving beyond the exegetical challenge of this part of the prayer to its practical application in everyday life, every person understands the concept of temptation. I would suggest that not a day passes when the average person isn't tempted in one way or another. Most of our daily temptations are what I call "small potatoes," the kinds of transgressions that plagued our thirteen-year-old in Chapter 4. We are tempted to be excessive with food or drink, to participate in the latest bit of juicy gossip, to undermine a coworker or lash out at a sibling or spouse. This list, as we all know, is endless. The temptations are real, and the damage of such sin can be substantial. It can lead to self-sabotage when it comes to physical, mental, emotional, and spiritual health; it can lead to broken relationships with friends, family, and associates; it can lead to social upheaval in our homes or places of work or even places of worship. To call this "small potatoes" is not to minimize the temptations or the sins, but to point the way to the deeper and underlying source of our weakness. Let's state it again: it is our pride and narcissism.

We have already discussed the "original sin" of Adam and Eve as found in the third chapter of Genesis. Their desire was to be like God, and they placed this desire above their commitment to be obedient to God. In the fourth chapter of Genesis we witness the inevitable descent into even greater disobedience that constitutes the downward spiral of pride and self-absorption. The two sons, Cain and Abel, had been born, and entering the world with them were the emotions associated with competition, pride, and envy. When God favored Abel's offering over that of Cain,

> *Cain was very angry, and his countenance*
> *fell. The LORD said to Cain, "Why are you*
> *angry, and why has your countenance*
> *fallen? If you do well, will you not be*
> *accepted? And if you do not do well, sin is*
> *lurking at the door; its desire is for you, but*
> *you must master it."*

(Genesis 4:5-7)

Reading this passage, one might say that God was helping Cain not to be "led into temptation." But God's warning was not enough to overcome Cain's pride. He invited Abel into the field, and there occurred the first of countless murders in the history of the human race.

The uncomfortable truth for all who read this bloody saga is that the root of all our sins against others lies in our pride. Gossip is not the same as murder, but it is initiated in the human heart by the same feelings of jealousy or pride or resentment. Review your personal list of temptations, either "small potatoes" or "big potatoes," and you will find that they generally rise out of a broken relationship with either God or another human being. In Christianity, of course, those two things are the same. Jesus is clear that we can't be in good relationship with God if we are alienated from brothers and sisters. Now consider the source of anger or alienation, and ask yourself if pride or narcissism plays a role. This is what the Bible means when it says the sins of the fathers will be passed to the children. It is not a genetic flaw so much as a learned response. The pride of Adam and Eve is the same that can be seen in Cain. With Cain, the temptation leads to murder, and the sordid history of sinful humanity begins to unfold.

Shame

Ironically, there is a form of temptation that is functionally the opposite of pride, but which is rooted in the same tenuous relationship with God, and that is often ignored in sermons and lectures on the topic. It is what I call self-denigration or self-hatred. It is the tendency to believe that you are terribly flawed in some way that is beyond the grace of God. It may strike the reader as odd to call this a sin, but in reality it is one of the ways in which we are less than faithful. Theologically, it is nothing less than distrusting the belief that the way God has made us is good enough. Good enough means that, if it is good enough for God, it should be good enough for us! In its extreme form, self-denigration can even be described as self-loathing. That particular word may sound somewhat hyperbolic, but if most people are utterly honest with themselves, they will discover that, at least at times, they carry with them a certain amount of shame or disgust or embarrassment about who they consider themselves to be. Biblically, this theme is certainly present in the story of Adam and Eve as they reached for the fruit of the tree of the knowledge of good and evil because they wanted to be more than God had created them to be. Then they experienced, in their nakedness, the devastating emotion of shame.

Brené Brown's March 2012 TED Talk, "Listening to Shame," has drawn more than six million viewers. She draws an important distinction between guilt and shame: guilt is feeling bad about what one has *done*; shame is feeling bad about who one *is*. The fact that this concept has resonated so powerfully with so many people confirms how debilitating the temptation can be.

The simple and most obvious example in today's world concerns body image. How many people look in the mirror and think, "Wow! God made me in a beautiful way. I am the right height, the right weight, and the right build. And look at how cute (or handsome) I am!" I would suggest that very few people are capable of doing this in a healthy, non-narcissistic way. The bitter truth is that we live in a society that overvalues physical appearance, and the response of most of us tends to be neurotic in one way or another.

A reasonable desire to be physically sound and to look one's best can reflect a perfectly normal and healthy self-image. In fact, it can grow out of the conviction that we believe ourselves to be the children of God and that "your body is a temple," as Paul expressed it in 1 Corinthians 6:19.

I affirm efforts to look one's best, to groom appropriately, and to take modest steps to maximize physical appearance. Warning signs arise when concern over appearance becomes extreme, or when it is driven out of some deep despair that "something is wrong with me." This is an issue that each person has the opportunity to confront and ponder. The hope is that such self-reflection will lead to both a healthier self-image and a deeper relationship with the One who created each of us.

The issue of self-denigration runs much deeper than concerns over body image. How many people, for instance, dwell on their belief that they aren't as smart as others or as socially competent or athletic or gifted? Through the years I have met with many, many people who have confessed that they believe God didn't really bless them with any significant gifts at all. At its extreme, this results in a person who wonders what place they deserve in the world or why they were born. In its more moderate manifestations, it leaves none of us untouched. I would be shocked if any readers have not at one time or another considered themselves to be flawed in some significant way.

To summarize, this kind of self-doubt can take many forms: concerns about physical or body image; doubts about mental or intellectual capacity; anxiety about emotional or spiritual stability; self-loathing over perceived moral shortcomings. The temptation to worry about any or all of these challenges is very real, and I am persuaded that Jesus wants us to avoid them along with the others that are more readily recognized and acknowledged. With this thought in mind, take a moment to recite the Lord's Prayer right now, and observe how meaningful this broader and deepened understanding of "temptations" can be.

All these temptations are rooted in our broken relationship with God, and all point to Paul's great theological innovation concerning the grace of God. Having read thus far, the biblically literate reader might return to Paul's difficult letter to the Romans, especially chapters 5–7, and try to discern anew the kind of frustration Paul had experienced throughout his life in trying to be fully obedient to the law. He had discovered that total fidelity to the law or to rules is not only impossible but that it leads to ever-increasing anxiety and sin. In his grace-filled relationship with Christ, Paul had discovered liberation from both anxiety and sin. At his best, he was able to accept the fact that he was perfectly made in the image of God, and that God's amazing grace had overcome his many perceived weaknesses and temptations. In fact, when he says "whenever I am weak, then I am strong" (2 Corinthians 12:10), he is referring to God's grace that makes him whole in spite of his spiritual flaws. The great Pauline conclusion is that a loving and grace-filled relationship with God is the only way in which the pride of Adam is defeated, and the only way in which we heal the pride and insecurity that lies at the root of all temptations.

Obsessive Thinking

There is one final form of temptation I want to discuss, and one that would never have occurred to me had I not begun the practice of meditation. If nothing else, spiritual practice will bring intense awareness to the amount of time a person spends obsessing about either the past or the future. When I encourage people to give meditation a try, the most common response a few days later is "It's impossible! I'm no good at this. I can't stop thinking!" Well, of course! That is precisely why mindfulness training is so powerful. It reveals to us the inner and oftentimes counterproductive ways that our minds work. Most people are shocked to realize how constantly their brain is "in gear," and especially how much of that time is devoted to thoughts about either the past or the future.

That brings us back to one of the ongoing themes of this book. The three aspects of time—past, present, and future—can be powerful allies in our efforts to lead hopeful and purposeful lives, but only if we appropriate them in positive ways. It is beneficial if we view the past as a foundational source of learning and wisdom, but the past has demonic power if we obsess over those things we cannot change. Similarly, the capacity to dream and envision the future is one of God's great gifts to human beings. It can be what motivates us and propels us forward on our physical and spiritual journeys. It can encourage us to do all sorts of wonderful things in the present. But it too has demonic power over our thoughts and spirits if we obsess over future outcomes we can't control.

A helpful term, often used in the field of psychology, describes the way many of us think about the future. Called "catastrophic thinking," it is the tendency to fantasize about future outcomes in a way that inevitably leads to the worst possible scenario. Consider this example: The parents of a high school junior discover that he not only has blown a mathematics exam but is failing English as well. They begin the process of catastrophic thinking by assuming that these current failing grades will lead to failure in his senior year and that failure in his senior year will cause the student to drop out of school. Knowing the statistics, the parents imagine that their high school dropout will not be able to get a good job, will then succumb to the temptation of drugs, and will finally end up incarcerated for criminal activity. The parents have succeeded in mentally sabotaging both themselves and their child by allowing anxiety to overtake their rationality.

If you do not see yourself in this example, there are numerous others that might be more relevant: waiting for the return of a medical test; experiencing turbulence in a marriage; receiving a less-than-excellent job performance review. All these and others can lead to chain-of-event thinking that consummates in a vision of disaster. Life, in its everyday challenges, presents us with many opportunities for catastrophic thinking.

It may be that some people, possessed of really positive mental genes and happy-go-lucky attitudes, rarely succumb to such temptations. But at one time or another, most of us have had powerful, existential experiences with this destructive way of thinking about the future. I confess that I personally have at times been so adept at this that I could have been nominated for the Catastrophic Thinking Hall of Fame.

The Present Moment

Obsessive thinking about either the past or the future can literally sap the joy and energy out of a person's life. The two statements I am about to make do not constitute exaggerations, so please pay close attention.

- People who continually obsess about the past will inevitably become depressed because they cannot change it.
- People who continually obsess about the future will inevitably become anxious because they cannot control it.

The way we understand and make the most of the three dimensions of time is crucially important to both our mental health and our spiritual vitality.

The person who decides to practice meditation or mindfulness training will not only discover the extent to which they reside mentally in either the past or the present, but also the liberating power of being in the present moment. Let me say clearly that this is not easy. Often I attempt to end a twenty-minute meditation by taking just three consecutive breaths without having any thoughts whatsoever. It sounds simple, but it is enormously challenging. One might say that our brains have minds of their own! But I want to encourage the reader who is so inclined to keep at it long enough to discover that, when it comes to meditation or spiritual practice, there is no such thing as failing. No matter how poorly one does it, it is an incredibly powerful tool for retraining the brain to remain calmer, more peaceful, and more at home in the present moment.

I am sure there are skeptics at this point, doubtful not only about the efficacy of meditation but also about its relevance to biblical teaching and the Lord's Prayer. Let me share a New Testament passage that led me to a more disciplined spiritual practice at a very challenging time in my life. One day I was reading, yet again, the great fourth chapter of Paul's letter to the Philippians, but it was as if I were reading it for the very first time:

> *Rejoice in the Lord always; again I will say,*
> *Rejoice. Let your gentleness be known to*
> *everyone. The Lord is near. Do not worry*
> *about anything, but in everything by prayer*
> *and supplication with thanksgiving let your*
> *requests be made known to God. And the*
> *peace of God, which surpasses all*

> *understanding, will guard your hearts and*
> *your minds in Christ Jesus.*
>
> (Philippians 4:4-7)

I was so struck by the unambiguous nature of Paul's statement: "Do not worry about anything." Paul was not suggesting this or making it a request. It comes in the form of a command. Is it true, I wondered, that God truly does not want me to worry about anything? Worrying, after all, is one of my gifts. I'm really good at worrying about things and also fixing them. Surely God isn't commanding me not to worry! The more I read and contemplated this passage—I actually printed it out and taped it to my computer—the more I realized I was not only an overly anxious worrier but also one who had embraced an attenuated relationship with God. It was daunting to admit that I truly did not trust God very much. I encourage the reader to review again the sixth chapter of Matthew, the story about Martha and Mary, and numerous other scriptures that encourage us to trust God more and ourselves less. We are commanded not to be anxious!

Here is a maxim that is true, powerful, and easy to remember: *The only place where we can experience God is in the present moment.* I have heard versions of that statement all my adult life, and yet I never fully understood it until I began spiritual practice and developed awareness of how consistently my brain focuses on either the past or the future. Once I started tuning in to the statement's fundamental truth, many biblical passages gained much more existential relevance for my life. The story of the Hebrews in the wilderness, for example, became a great paradigm of what it means to live faithfully. I heard anew the words of Jesus when he said, "Martha, Martha, you are worried and distracted by many things....Mary has chosen the better part" (Luke 10:41-42) or "So do not worry about tomorrow, for tomorrow will bring worries of its own" (Matthew 6:34).

One reason we enjoy a spectacular sunset or sunrise, a great view of the Grand Canyon, or the flight of an eagle is that those sights force us to be in the present. The same can be true about times when wonderful music captures our full auditory attention. These kinds of experiences are powerful precisely because of their ability to transport us out of the past or future into the now. That is one reason why we so often explain these moments as experiencing the presence of God. More properly understood, God is not becoming present to us in these experiences, but by being in the moment, we are becoming aware of God.

In the Paths of Righteousness

When I ask God to "lead us not into temptation," I often think of the Twenty-third Psalm. I don't know whether Jesus had it in mind when he taught the Lord's Prayer to the disciples, but the words *lead us* invite a compelling comparison to the most beloved of all the Psalms. One might say that this psalm states in a more positive way the same thoughts that Jesus was encouraging for the disciples:

The LORD is my shepherd, I shall not want.
He makes me lie down in green pastures;
he leads me beside still waters;
he restores my soul.
He leads me in right paths
for his name's sake.

Even though I walk through the darkest valley,
I fear no evil;
for you are with me;
your rod and your staff—
they comfort me.

You prepare a table before me
in the presence of my enemies;
you anoint my head with oil;
my cup overflows.
Surely goodness and mercy shall follow me
all the days of my life,
and I shall dwell in the house of the LORD
my whole life long.

This is an extraordinary image of the Lord *leading us* beside still waters, *leading us* in the paths of righteousness, *leading us* through times when we are surrounded by enemies, *leading us* gracefully to our final moments on earth. I encourage contemplation of these images, and perhaps even recitation of the Twenty-third Psalm, as a way of developing a richer and more robust understanding of the closing phrases of the Lord's Prayer.

The Doxology

For thine is the kingdom, and the power, and the glory, forever.

The final phrase of the Lord's Prayer, known as the doxology, is not found in most translations of Matthew's Gospel and was undoubtedly not part of the original text. It was added to the prayer by some in the early Christian community and is first found in the Didache (also known as The Teaching of the Twelve Apostles), an early Christian treatise. Throughout the centuries, the Lord's Prayer has been both prayed and written with and without the doxology, depending on the traditions and customs of the particular community of faith. That remains true today, and though it has always been recited in my own tradition, it is historically accurate to consider it an optional part of the prayer, but one that is not necessarily unimportant for those who embrace it as part of their tradition and practice.

I confess that for most of my life I have thought of this closing phrase as merely a snappy sign-off for the prayer. That mistaken understanding perhaps begins early in life. Listen to a group of typical five-year-olds who have recently learned the prayer, and they will often rip this phrase off quickly as they experience the adrenaline rush of having reached the finish line in their race to recite it flawlessly. But is the doxology really just a sign-off, or did the early church place it there for a reason?

As I have thought about the prayer with more intentionality over the past few years, I have come to the conclusion that, for those who pray it, the doxology is a perfect way of concluding the prayer. It effectively closes the circle that was begun with the opening phrase. Recall that "Our Father, who art in heaven, hallowed be thy name" begins the prayer by acknowledging the transcendence of God. It places us on our knees as supplicants before a creator God who is bigger than we can imagine, and we take our rightful place as those who make humble entreaty to God. This tone sets the relationship that characterizes the rest of the prayer, and the doxology reinforces it.

There is a way of saying the doxology that helps make it a reinforcing statement for the entire message. Try reciting the doxology with the following emphasis: "For *thine* is the kingdom, and *thine* is the power, and *thine* is the glory forever." This way of saying the doxology underscores the fact that the prayer isn't about me but about God. It's not *my* kingdom but *God's* kingdom, not *my* power but *God's* power, not *my* glory but *God's* glory. It all belongs to God. It is the perfect antidote for our ongoing temptation to be prideful or to make it all about us. And it is a final reminder that we live always in the powerful presence of God's overwhelming grace: the grace that makes us whole in spite of everything that makes us broken.

Spiritual Reflection: Dealing with Temptation

I remember an early spring morning, about a year after I became committed to daily spiritual practice, when I enjoyed an unusually rich time of prayer and meditation on the patio of our backyard. It was still dark when I finally rose and in a state of near ecstasy walked through the French doors leading to our breakfast room and immediately banged my knee hard into a breakfast table chair. The X-rated expletive that immediately flew out of my mouth was, shall we say, not consistent with the prayer time that had preceded that moment. In a split second I had taken the day back for myself and cursed the moment that preceded the rising sun rather than blessing it. This is the fallen humanity we all deal with, and it does not go away just because we participate in spiritual practice. Temptation is our constant companion!

I share this story to counterbalance any perception that spiritual practice leads to any kind of spiritual superiority. On the contrary, spiritual practice has granted me an invitation to be more authentic and honest about my shortcomings and temptations, and there is something liberating about that. I fully believe that if one is to accept the challenge of daily spiritual practice, it will in no way lead to a sense of spiritual attainment or superiority, but rather the opposite. Spiritual practice is like looking at yourself honestly in the mirror: you see the good, the bad, and the ugly. Liberation comes in knowing that God sees it all as well and yet loves us unconditionally. It really is only when we can perceive and embrace our fallen humanity that we can fully accept and embrace the gift of God's amazing grace and love.

I close by returning to the dictum I have articulated from the pulpit of my church many times, one that I believe drives home the most important decision any person can ever make. Either God is or God isn't. It is just that simple. You don't get any other choices. And the choice you make will determine how you live your life. It will influence how you do your work, how you raise your children, how you relate to friends and family. It is a choice that, one way or the other, will leave nothing untouched. Yet, it is a choice that remains largely ignored by most modern people. Not only atheists and agnostics, but many of us who are nominally Christian, get up and live each day without giving much thought to the question of God. The challenges of modern scientific discovery have made contemplation of that question uncomfortable. Still, it is the ultimate question about the meaning and purpose of life itself. To ignore it is to forfeit the existential power of living an examined life.

Reciting the Lord's Prayer daily is a powerful way of answering that question every single day. Either God is or God isn't. Either this day belongs to God or it doesn't. Either my life is ultimately in the hands of God or it isn't. Praying the prayer that Jesus taught not only helps us rediscover great biblical truths; it can provide a daily moment of truth in which we make a conscious commitment to live the powerful and joyous life of faith.

Notes

1. "The Lord's Prayer–From the Ritual of the Former Methodist Church," *The United Methodist Hymnal* (Nashville: The United Methodist Publishing House, 1989), #895.
2. John Ortberg, *God Is Closer Than You Think* (2005; repr., Grand Rapids: Zondervan, 2014), 176.
3. Dorothy Day, *The Duty of Delight: The Diaries of Dorothy Day* (Milwaukee: Marquette University, 2011), 519, quoted in David Brooks, *The Road to Character* (New York: Random House, 2015), 2.
4. C. S. Lewis, *Mere Christianity* (New York: HarperCollins, 1952), quoted in Michael Gerson, "The GOP Needs to Learn that Character Matters (June 16, 2016). http://www.gazettextra.com/20160616/michael_gerson_the_gop_needs_to_learn_that_character_matters.
5. Douglas R. A. Hare, *Matthew.* (Louisville: John Knox Press, 1993), 69–70.

Acknowledgments

Anyone who writes a book becomes deeply aware of how many people have influenced its content either directly or indirectly. Thus, the challenge of publicly thanking individuals becomes rather daunting. But some people must be named, and I do so with the expectation—or perhaps simply the hope—of grace from those who accidentally have been left out.

Matt Thompson is the young man who coached me into experimentation with meditation and a more contemplative style of prayer. The approach to this book, along with many of its insights, would not have taken place without his nudging. This is a story about how God can work through the powerful whispers of friends and family. I am indebted to Father Richard Rohr, whose daily e-mail meditations have fed me both intellectually and spiritually. There is no doubt that his thoughts and perspective have influenced the way I look at both life and ministry. I am also a regular reader of *New York Times* columnist David Brooks. His weekly columns and his last two books, one of which I cite in Chapter 3, have kept me intellectually engaged. In recent years he has written profoundly about his own evolving spiritual journey.

Without a very supportive staff, some of whom I have had the joy of working with for many years, this book would not have been possible. Cathy Sweeney, in particular, provided valuable feedback and insights as we neared the final draft. Dr. Alyce McKenzie, my good friend and preaching coach, reviewed the manuscript for theological soundness and in the process also provided superb editing advice. My editor at Abingdon Press, Ron Kidd, was not only a joy to work with, but inevitably prompted me and pointed me in very productive ways. It was the perfect partnership.

Perhaps the ones who deserve the most credit for the book are the members and worshiping visitors at Christ United Methodist Church in Plano, Texas. Their attentive ears, their probing questions, and their personal faith stories have fed me and kept me alive both intellectually and spiritually. There is no way to overstate their contributions to anything I have said or written through the years.

Finally, thanks to my wife Bobby (Baba), my children, and my grandchildren for their enduring patience. They know me so well, and yet they still put up with me, which is surely an ongoing expression of the power of grace. May it be so for us all.